Short Bike Rides™
on Cape Cod, Nantucket, & the Vineyard

"Nantucket, Martha's Vineyard, and Cape Cod are ideally suited for bicyclists. . . . The book provides detailed directions, route maps, and tells what you'll see along the way."
—*The Boston Globe*

"Keeps you organized and informed as you pedal through the back roads."
—*Women's Sports and Fitness* magazine

"Contains . . . rides that allow you to experience, up close, this beloved landscape in all its diversity—from beaches to bogs, kettleponds to pine forests, bustling towns to vast solitary moors and sweeping ocean vistas."
—*Ideas for Better Living* magazine

"The directions allow little chance of getting lost—except in the scenery."
—*Cape Cod Life*

SHORT BIKE RIDES SERIES

Short Bike Rides™
on
Cape Cod, Nantucket, & the Vineyard

Sixth Edition

By
Edwin Mullen and Jane Griffith

An East Woods Book

The Globe Pequot Press

Old Saybrook, Connecticut

Copyright © 1994, 1997 by Edwin Mullen
Copyright © 1977, 1984, 1988, 1991 by Edwin Mullen and Jane Griffith

Library of Congress Cataloging-in-Publication Data
Mullen, Edwin.
    Short bike rides on Cape Cod, Nantucket, & the Vineyard / by Edwin Mullen and Jane Griffith. — 6th ed.
        p.   cm. — (Short bike rides series)
    "An East Woods book."
    ISBN 0-7627-0075-0
    1. Bicycle touring—Massachusetts—Cape Cod—Guidebooks.
    2. Bicycle touring—Massachusetts—Nantucket Island—Guidebooks.
    3. Bicycle touring—Massachusetts—Martha's Vineyard—Guidebooks.
    4. Cape Cod (Mass.)—Guidebooks. 5. Nantucket Island (Mass.)—
    Guidebooks. 6. Martha's Vineyard (Mass.)—Guidebooks.
    I. Griffith, Jane. II. Title. III. Series.
    GV1045.5.M42C364   1997
    796.6'4'074492—dc20   96-41635
                                                                            CIP

♻ This book is printed on recycled paper.
Manufactured in the United States of America
Sixth Edition/First Printing

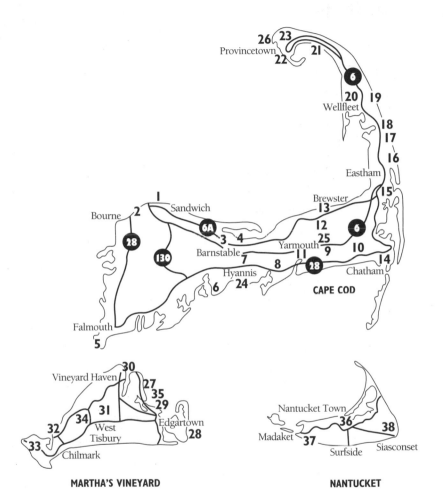

26 23
Provincetown
22 21
6
20 19
Wellfleet
18
17
16
Eastham
15
Brewster
1
Sandwich 13
Bourne 2 12
6A 6
3 4 25
Yarmouth 9
28 Barnstable 7 11 10
130 8 28 14
Hyannis Chatham
6 24
CAPE COD
Falmouth
5

30
Vineyard Haven
27
35
29
34 31
32 West Edgartown
Tisbury 28
33
Chilmark

Nantucket Town
36 38
Madaket 37
Surfside Siasconset

MARTHA'S VINEYARD   **NANTUCKET**

Contents

MARTHA'S VINEYARD

NANTUCKET

Introduction

This book combines two pleasurable experiences: riding a bicycle and exploring Cape Cod ("the Cape") and the islands of Martha's Vineyard and Nantucket. Three of the most visited places in America, they are very small but there is magic in them, a gift from Nature and from the people who've been coming here since the early seventeenth century. Some of the finest beaches in the United States are here, 300 miles of them, and salt marshes, magnificent sand dunes, lakes (called ponds), farms, pine forests, little harbors with their boats (sail and motor, very large ones and very small ones, with even more in between, sailing into or out of the harbor or swinging gracefully at anchor), family restaurants and fancy ones, farms and moors, villages, museums, and artists and their works—all surrounded by the sea, from which come the fish and oysters and lobsters that grace the tables of the innumerable restaurants and inns.

The best way to enjoy all of this is by bicycle. It will take a little longer to get where you want to go, but as you ride, you see everything and have the time to take in the full beauty of the sights, sounds, and scents that surround you. If you bring your own bicycle, be sure to include a handlebar bag and two pannier bags for the rack on the back. If you decide to rent, bring the bags along. Some of the rental shops have rear racks, but if yours doesn't, you will have at least a handlebar bag for the book, your wallet, and whatever else you can stuff in: sandwiches, bathing suit and small towel, and so on.

To ensure your enjoyment, take the precautions outlined in the section on safety. As for the bike itself, I now recommend one of the twenty-one-speed mountain/road bikes that have fat and deep-treaded tires and a lighter frame than their mountain cousins. They do not track as well as the usual touring bike with narrow, high-pressure tires, and drop bars, but for seeing the countryside, the more upright posture afforded by the hybrid is better, and for the occasional dirt road or a sudden swerve onto a grass or dirt shoulder, it is hard to beat. And the extra gears combined with the latest Shimano click-click shifters are marvelous!

Cape Cod

This arm of Massachusetts, site of the Pilgrims' first landfall, is about 75 miles long and has more than 300 miles of coastline. Formed some 10,000 years ago by action of the retreating glacier, the Cape is a bony, sandy outcropping punctuated by bluffs, marshes, and ponds (probably created when dense ice chunks amid the debris melted away).

The Cape was settled within a couple of decades of Plymouth, and the colonists took to fishing, hunting, and haying the salt meadows. Settlers also denuded the Cape of its trees for housing, shipbuilding, firewood, and pastureland. The cutting over, combined with the natural wash and blow-dry that the flora and terrain absorb from relentless waves and winds, explains the Cape's unique and fascinating appearance: rugged but right.

Cape Cod National Seashore

The Cape Cod National Seashore was created in 1961 by an act of Congress. Its 27,000 acres, located in six towns, are under National Parks Service supervision. About two-thirds of the acres are owned by the Seashore; the rest of the acreage remains in private hands or is held by the towns, but physical changes to these properties are strictly controlled.

The two visitors' centers, Salt Pond and Province Lands, are open seven days a week from spring until early winter. Salt Pond offers an illuminated tabletop map of the Cape, several films and dioramas illustrating the history and geology of the Cape, and trail guides and facilities. Province Lands Visitors' Center provides one of the Cape's most beautiful overlooks. Trail guides, exhibits, orientation talks, and rest rooms are available. Camping is not allowed in the Seashore. The dunes, flora, and fauna must remain undisturbed. Lifeguard service and public rest rooms are available at the following beaches: Coast Guard, Nauset Light, Marconi, Head of Meadow, Race Point, and Herring Cove. The Seashore extends along the Cape's entire Atlantic shore, from its southernmost point below Chatham to Provincetown. Unforgettable! For more information about the Cape, I heartily recommend that you get a copy of the *Guide to Cape Cod* by Frederick

Pratson, available at bookstores or from The Globe Pequot Press, P.O. Box 833, Old Saybrook, CT 06475–0833.

Martha's Vineyard

One of the truths of the theater is that contrast is the essence of drama. And so it is with an island—the contrast between a speck of land, surrounded by the constantly moving water, and the mainland, anchored to the distant horizon. I was born on an island and still feel its influence, but you don't have to be born on an island to feel and enjoy its uniqueness; simply crossing the sea to reach it will do. As your ferry approaches, you watch the island looming ahead, growing ever larger as you enter the harbor and prepare to dock. The entire ship vibrates as its propellers go into reverse for the docking, accompanied by the sights and sounds of clanking chains and swirling water. And when the ship is secure at last, the gates go up and you step ashore onto your island—Martha's Vineyard!

In 1602 wild grapes grew abundantly on the island, and in that year explorer Bartholomew Gosnold, who had a young daughter named Martha, made this vineyard her namesake.

Colonists came in 1642 to establish Edgartown, having bought the entire island, unbeknownst to the Indian inhabitants who had lived there compatibly from time immemorial, for £40 from two gentlemen in England. The community prospered with fishing, whaling, sheep herding, dairying, and boat building, and new settlements were established. The Revolution disrupted the islanders' lives and economy, but recovery was complete by 1820, when the whaling and building booms were at their height. The triple blow of the Gold Rush, the Civil War, and the discovery of petroleum would have resulted in a bleak future indeed had it not been for the timely burgeoning of summer religious camp meetings, which prompted a land development boom. To this day tourism is the island's principal source of income, causing the population to soar from some 7,000 year-round residents to about 70,000 in the summer.

With that in mind, we exhort you not to bring a car here in the summer. Congestion is terrible, and parking is ridiculous. From May through September—and even into October—the bike's the thing! Bring your own or rent one, and take the bus between treks. Shuttle buses run on the hour out of Vineyard Haven and on the half-hour out of Edgartown via Oak Bluffs mid-May through October. Buses stop on Union Street in Vineyard Haven, at the traffic circle in Oak Bluffs, and at the courthouse in Edgartown. They run from 8:00 A.M. to 10:00 P.M. in the summer, 8:00 A.M. to 6:00 P.M. in the spring and fall. If, however, you have to take your vehicle, call the Steam Ship Authority at (508) 477–8600 for an advance reservation.

Ferries sail from Woods Hole to Vineyard Haven year-round and to Oak Bluffs between June 16 and September 16. Boats also come from New Bedford, Falmouth, and Hyannis in the summer (June through September). Those from Falmouth and Hyannis dock only at Oak Bluffs and don't carry automobiles. After September 30 there's no service to Oak Bluffs. Note: The ferry from Woods Hole to Oaks Bluff does carry vehicles.

If that's confusing, you can check with the Steamship Authority (508–477–8600) and/or Hy-Line, foot passengers only, in Hyannis (508–778–2600).

No camping is allowed on the beaches. There are two commercial campgrounds, one in Vineyard Haven, one in Oak Bluffs. Alcoholic beverages are sold in Oak Bluffs and Edgartown; the rest of the island is dry, but you can bring your own. Beaches open to the public include the following: in Vineyard Haven, Owen Park Beach; in Oak Bluffs, Joseph Sylvia State Beach and the Town Beach; in Edgartown, Katama (South) Beach; in Chappaquiddick, East Beach; in Chilmark, Menemsha Town Beach and Menemsha Hills; and in Gay Head, Lobsterville Beach. The Martha's Vineyard State Forest Bike Trail provides the cyclist with 14 miles of bike paths around and through this 4,000-acre pine, oak, and spruce forest.

Nantucket

Nantucket, 30 miles south of Cape Cod, was created when the great ice age glacier melted away and dropped the immense load of earth and debris that shaped the island's width and length of 3 miles by 15.

Gosnold, Martha's Vineyard discoverer, also came here in 1602, but the island wasn't settled until some sixty years later, when the Quakers came. The Indians were kindly disposed, which was apparently unfortunate for them: By the middle 1800s they had left or died off, and their culture vanished from Nantucket.

From 1712, when the first sperm whale was done in, until the middle 1800s, when the Fire of 1846 gutted the town and combined with the Civil War and the period's economic developments to end the bubble, Nantucket prospered, and the whaling captains built their Georgian, Federal, and Greek Revival mansions, leaving some 400 houses here that are more than a hundred years old.

Nantucket's present economy depends largely on tourism, but commercial fishing is still a significant activity. In a unique way Nantucket depends on the past to attract people here and depends on the present to keep them coming. The island's exotic whaling history captures the imagination, but its sun, sand, flora, and moors bring one sharply into the present.

Reach Nantucket by ferry from Woods Hole, summer only (3½ hours) or Hyannis year-round (2½ hours). I urge you not to take a car here. It is a small island; you'll have a time finding a place to park on it, and the entire island is exuberantly and easily reached by bicycle. (Bring your own or rent one here.) If, however, you must bring your vehicle, call the Steam Ship Authority at (508) 477–8600 for an advance reservation. Nantucket doesn't allow camping out or sleeping in vehicles. Public beaches are Jetties Beach, Surfside, Cisco, Sconset, Dionis, and Madaket.

Safety

Riding the roads of Cape Cod and the islands on a bicycle can be dangerous. Observe all Massachusetts state bicycle and vehicle laws. Always ride with the traffic flow, not against it. (Many's the time while riding to work in New Haven I've been faced with an oncoming bicyclist on a one-way street or coming at me on the wrong side of a two-way street.)

Stop at red lights and stop signs. Ride defensively. Be wary of motorists, all of them! They probably don't see you, and a fender bender to them is a leg buster or worse to the cyclist.

Be visible at night, and wear a helmet—doing so reduces your risk of serious injury in an accident by 75 percent.

Give clear hand signals. Yield to pedestrians. Ride single file. Don't ride on sidewalks in town centers. Walk your bike when going against traffic on a one-way street. Call out and slow down when approaching horses. Check your bike before beginning a trip. Make sure that all nuts are tight and that the derailleurs and brakes are working properly. No matter how long you have been riding, use a checklist before each ride.

Checklist
 1. Brakes
 2. Derailleurs
 3. Wheel nuts
 4. Tires
 5. Lights
 6. Reflectors and rear-view mirror
 7. Bolt-cutter-proof lock
 8. Tool kit
 9. Front and rear bags
10. Small first-aid kit
11. Helmet
12. Sunglasses
13. Sunscreen
14. Wash'n Dri towelettes
15. Water bottle

Now that you're ready to start out, I'd like to thank you for buying my book to explore these magical lands with, and I'd like to invite you to write me at any time with your comments, complaints, suggestions, observations—whatever you like. Write to me, Edwin Mullen, c/o Globe Pequot Press, 6 Business Park Road, P.O. Box 833, Old Saybrook, CT 06475.

Godspeed—and may the wind be always at your back!

Cape Cod Canal–Sandwich

Number of miles:	17
Approximate pedaling time:	2¼ hours
Terrain:	Flat
Surface:	Good
Things to see:	Sandwich Glass Museum, Dexter Grist Mill, Hoxie House, Heritage Plantation, Shawme Pond, glassblowers at the Pairpoint Crystal factory

This lovely and varied ride starts at the Cape Cod Canal, just under the Bourne Bridge. There is a parking lot here, and rest rooms (during the summer season only) maintained by the U.S. Army Corps of Engineers. Mount up and turn right onto the paved road, which runs along the canal. This road is for government vehicles (a rare sight), strollers, in-line skaters, and bicycles only.

Follow the contour of the canal, which, in the warm months, is full of boats, large and small. The current is swift—6 to 7 knots at times—and often the sailboats seem to be standing still. Near the end of the canal, you'll come to the NEPCO electrical power generating plant. Skirt around it on the canal side to the new Bulkhead Recreation Area, which marks the end of the access-road-cum-bike-path. A pause here may be in order at one of the picnic tables facing the canal. When you're ready to continue, go right onto Freezer Road, which borders the East Boat Basin and the parking lot of the Cape Cod Canal Marina, and then continue the circuit of the boat basin by turning left onto Ed Moffitt Drive and then making a right at the T with Gallo and a quick left onto Town Neck Road, which should take you to the end of the canal itself. The U.S. Army Corps of Engineers

No. 1 Cape Cod Canal–Sandwich

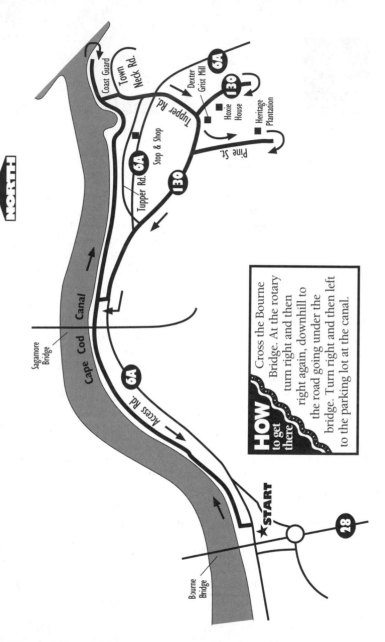

NORTH

Sagamore Bridge

Cape Cod Canal

Coast Guard
Town Neck Rd.

6A
130

Dexter Grist Mill

Tupper Rd.

Stop & Shop

Tupper Rd. 6A

Hoxie House

Heritage Plantation

130

Pine St.

Access Rd. 6A

Bourne Bridge

★ START

28

HOW to get there

Cross the Bourne Bridge. At the rotary turn right and then right again, downhill to the road going under the bridge. Turn right and then left to the parking lot at the canal.

has built another recreation area here, called the Sandcatcher Recreation Area, complete with rest rooms. If you like, you can continue on to the tip of the entrance to the canal, where there is a beach. When my thirteen-year-old daughter and I first rode this part of the ride late in the fall of 1976, the moon was rising over Cape Cod Bay, the navigation lights were flashing, and we could make out the buoys marking the entrance to the canal. 'Twas a beautiful sight!

Turn around and come back along the roadway to Coast Guard Road. Turn left and go past the Coast Guard Station on your right. At the stop sign turn right onto Town Neck Road. Just over the railroad tracks, come to a T with Tupper Road. Turn left onto Tupper. There is a bike path here, alongside the road. Stay on Tupper past Route 6A to the tiny center of Sandwich.

The Dexter Grist Mill was built around 1650 and still grinds cornmeal. The Hoxie House, a classic saltbox, was built in 1637, which makes it the oldest house on Cape Cod. It was acquired by the town and beautifully restored. Both the Dexter Grist Mill and the Hoxie House are open from mid-June through September. Shawme Pond is a jewel of a pond, teeming with wild geese, ducks, and swans in season. It is an artificial lake, created around 1633 when settlers built a dam to provide water power for the mill. In April the fish ladder is packed with thousands of leaping herring (alewives) coming upstream to spawn.

After you have enjoyed all of these goodies (and if you have some time and a few dollars left), turn around and head north on Route 130. In about a mile you come to Pine Street. Turn left and go uphill for 0.6 mile until you come to Heritage Plantation. This is a large place, dedicated to antique America. It consists of beautiful gardens, a working windmill, a 1912 carousel, a round Shaker barn, antique automobiles, and so on. Hours are 10:00 A.M. to 4:00 P.M. from May 13 to mid-October.

When you are ready to leave, return (downhill this time) to Route 130. Turn left on 130, past an old sprawling cemetery on the right, past Shawme-Crowell State Park—one of two on Cape Cod with campsites (first come, first served!). When you arrive at the junction with 6A, go left onto it; you have to turn right and then left to do so.

At the fork of Routes 6A and 6, bear right where the sign says ROUTE 6 AND SAGAMORE VILLAGE. Ride through Sagamore Village on the sidewalk and you'll soon see the Sagamore Bridge ahead, arching over your road as it crosses over the canal. Just before the bridge, on the right, is Pairpoint Crystal, America's oldest glassworks, where hand-blown crystal glassware has been produced since 1837 and is still being produced today by glassblowers using tools and techniques developed by Deming Jarves at Sandwich Glass more than one hundred years ago.

You can watch the glassblowers practicing their ancient craft Monday through Friday from 9:00 A.M. to 4:30 P.M. The showroom is open Monday through Saturday from 9:00 A.M. to 6:00 P.M. and Sunday from 10:00 A.M. to 6:00 P.M. And if you've never been in one of the ubiquitous Christmas Tree stores, there's a big one across from the Pairpoint Crystal factory, up a short, steep road. These unique emporiums accept out-of-state checks—perhaps because they're a regular stop for tour buses. The Sagamore Bridge is but a few hundred feet from the glass factory. Here you turn right and make your way to the canal road, where you turn left and retrace your route the 3.3 miles back to the Bourne Bridge.

Bourne

Number of miles:	18.5
Approximate pedaling time:	2¼ hours
Terrain:	Varied—long flat stretches, some hills
Surface:	Good
Things to see:	Cape Cod Canal, Cataumet Methodist Church, Aptucxet Trading Post and Windmill, communities of Bourne, Monument Beach, Pocasset

The town of Bourne, once part of Sandwich, was incorporated in 1854; however, its share of this magical land and sea is timeless. It embraces the land on both sides of the Cape Cod Canal, which was first carved out of the land in the early 1900s as a private business venture financed by August Belmont to give ships a safe passage, away from the storms and shoals of the Cape. It was too narrow, however, allowing only one-way passage. Mr. Belmont lost money on his canal, the federal government bought it in 1928, and the U.S. Army Corps of Engineers took over. They made it deeper and wider and straightened it out, and they even had the Bourne and Sagamore bridges built. Now it's the world's widest sea-level canal, and the first part of this ride takes you along its southeastern section.

The ride begins in the parking lot on the east side of the canal, under the Bourne Bridge. There are picnic tables and rest rooms here. These facilities, as well as the canal and its "Tow Path," are maintained by the U.S. Army Corps of Engineers; however, the rest rooms are open in the summer season only. Mount up and go left on the paved Canal Service Road, heading south. After a mile, at the site of the railroad bridge, you'll reach the end of this leg. Walk your bike

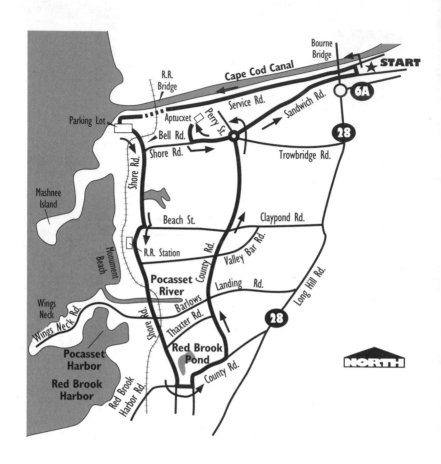

No. 2 Bourne

HOW to get there — Cross the Bourne Bridge. At the rotary turn right and then right again, downhill to the road going under the bridge. Turn right and then left to the parking lot at the canal.

down the embankment and over the tracks to the parking lot. Ride through the lot and alongside the canal on Jefferson Street to the point; here you're almost at the south end of the canal.

Now retrace the route to the parking lot; turn right on Bell Road, which may not have a street sign; and ride out to Shore Road. Turn right on Shore Road. Here you begin your exploration of the western shore of the upper Cape, winding your way down to the border of North Falmouth. Bear left at the fork, where there is a small traffic island. Pass Old Dam Road on the left. At a sign that points to POCAS-SET—2 MILES, Shore Road appears to come to a T; in fact, it jogs right and then left in front of the railroad station and a Cumberland Farms store. Continue on Shore Road. You're now in the community of Monument Beach. Upon reaching the Pocasset River, stop at the bridge and take a look at the boats. This is a colorful, picturesque scene. There's a tiny harbor, but evidently the draft is deep, because there are some enormous boats moored here. This area is called Pocasset.

Continue on Shore Road past Barlow's Landing. Just before going under an overpass, you'll see a sign to the Marine Center on your right. Ride in for a look at the boats and beautiful Red Brook Harbor (if you like boats, that is). Then go under the overpass and up the hill—which is the first real hill we've encountered on this ride.

Turn left onto Red Brook Harbor Road, then turn left onto County Road. Soon you'll see the Cataumet Methodist Church and cemetery. The building dates from 1765. At the fork with Long Hill Road, bear left, staying on County Road. In 2 more miles, after a couple of significant uphill grades, you'll reach a six-way intersection where there will be signs to PROVIDENCE–BOSTON–MONUMENT BEACH. Turn left on Shore Road. You'll be able to see the Aptucxet Windmill and Trading Post from Shore Road. Turn right onto Aptucxet Road and head for the windmill. Just beyond it is the Aptucxet Trading Post. The present building is a replica erected on the foundation of the original trading post, which was built in 1627 and carried on a three-way trading among the Dutch who sailed up from New York, the Pilgrims, and the Native Americans of Cape Cod and the Wampanoag Federation. The medium of trade was wampum, bits of polished quahog clamshells. There is a modest charge for the tour, which is offered from April 1 to October 31.

After your visit come back to Shore Road, turn left, return to the intersection, and take Sandwich Road back to your starting place at the Bourne Bridge.

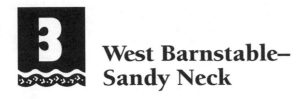

West Barnstable–
Sandy Neck

Number of miles:	10.3
Approximate pedaling time:	1 hour
Terrain:	Varied
Surface:	Good
Things to see:	Old Village Store, West Parish Meetinghouse, Sandy Neck, Great Marshes

West Barnstable is one of the many villages that constitute the town of Barnstable. (Some of the other villages you'll be exploring are Centerville, Craigville, Osterville, Hyannis, and Hyannis Port.) One of the marvels you'll experience along this ride are the sand dunes at Sandy Neck, which are 6 miles long and 0.5 mile wide. The great marshes of Barnstable are sheltered by these dunes, which began to form about 3,500 years ago.

After you have parked your bike "carrier" or have arrived on your rented bike at the starting place on Route 149, just off Route 6A, between the little railroad station and the Old Village Store, pay a visit to the latter. It has excellent cheese for a roadside snack, and you'll enjoy poking around the old store.

To start the ride, turn right on Meetinghouse Way (149) and go uphill. At the crest you'll get a view across the Great Marshes. Along this two-lane country road is a sidewalk that you can use. In about a mile you'll come to a fork with a road going off at forty-five degrees to your right. It is just before a large sign saying 6 WEST–BUZZARD'S BAY–BOSTON EXIT AHEAD. Turn right before the sign, going past the West Parish Meetinghouse on your left. You are on Cedar Street. Pass Willow Street, Gemini Drive, and Cedarcrest Lane. The next is Maple Street, 0.7 mile from the meetinghouse; turn right. This is a gently

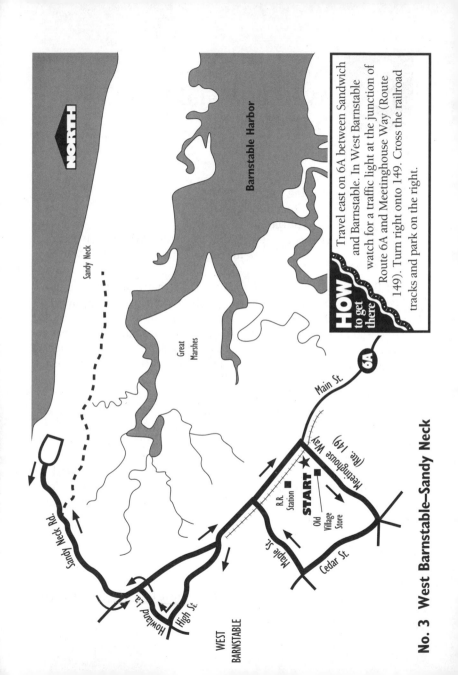

HOW to get there

Travel east on 6A between Sandwich and Barnstable. In West Barnstable watch for a traffic light at the junction of Route 6A and Meetinghouse Way (Route 149). Turn right onto 149. Cross the railroad tracks and park on the right.

NORTH

Barnstable Harbor

Sandy Neck

Great Marshes

Sandy Neck Rd.

Howland La.

High St.

WEST BARNSTABLE

Maple St.

Cedar St.

R.R. Station

Old Village Store

START

Meetinghouse Way (Rte. 149)

Main St.

6A

No. 3   West Barnstable–Sandy Neck

rolling country road. Cross the railroad tracks and turn left on 6A.

Your route parallels the Great Marshes here. This extensive marsh comprises 3,000 acres. The early settlers used the "salt hay" collected here for such varied purposes as fodder, bedding, compost, thatching, and insulation. If you're ever wondering what all those little wooden boxes are that dot such areas, your curiosity can now be satisfied: They are bird houses for tree swallows attracted to the marsh to eat insects and wooden traps for horseflies (see Hugh and Heather Sadlier's *Short Walks on Cape Cod and the Vineyard,* The Globe Pequot Press).

Proceed on 6A to the fork with High Street. Bear left up High Street and enjoy another view of the Great Marshes. When you come to Howland Lane, turn right and rejoin 6A by turning left.

In short order turn right on Sandy Neck Road. Ride past marshes and sand dunes to the parking lot. From there you can go swimming, hiking, or birding on the marked trails winding through the 6 miles of Sandy Neck dunes. The beach, being on the bay side of the Cape, is a pebbly one but nevertheless beautiful and inviting. This site is formally called Scortin Neck Beach and Nature Recreation Area. When you are ready, return to 6A on Sandy Neck Road. Turn left and proceed on 6A until you come to Meetinghouse Way. Turn right and return to your vehicle in the railroad parking lot.

4

Barnstable–Cummaquid

Number of miles:	10.8
Approximate pedaling time:	1 hour
Terrain:	Gently rolling
Surface:	Good
Things to see:	Barnstable County Court House, Sturgis Library, Trayser Memorial Museum

Now you are in the village of Barnstable of the town of Barnstable, and there is much to see and savor. The Sturgis Library, whose small parking lot serves as your starting place, can be a quiet (library-style) and restful respite when you finish the ride.

Come out of the library parking lot and head east on 6A (also called Cranberry Highway). You'll soon pass the Barnstable Comedy Club, which is an amateur theater, and the Barnstable County Court House. This building, completed in 1774, houses exhibits of flags and paintings. A film depicting Cape Cod's history is presented. Visitors are welcome on weekdays from 1:30 to 4:30 P.M. Route 6A is very busy here and very narrow. There is a sidewalk on the left, and we recommend its use when there are no pedestrians.

About 2 miles from the start of the ride, you'll pass the post office in the tiny community of Cummaquid. Turn left on Keveney Lane and head toward Mill Creek and Hallet's Mill Pond, going downhill. When you cross the bridge, you enter a corner of Yarmouth Port, and Keveney Lane becomes Mill Lane. The view of the marsh and Anthony's Cummaquid Inn is impressive. Water Street goes off to the left shortly after crossing the bridge. Continue on Mill Lane. Return to 6A and turn right, heading back to Barnstable.

If you have time, when you get to Route 6 on Mill Lane, turn left

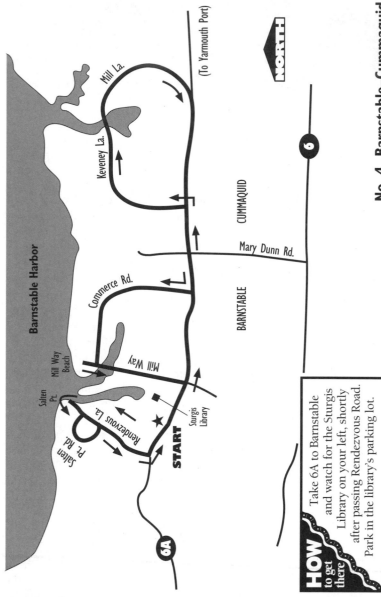

Barnstable Harbor

Mill La.

Keveney La.

(To Yarmouth Port)

NORTH

Commerce Rd.

CUMMAQUID

Mary Dunn Rd.

BARNSTABLE

Mill Way Beach

Mill Way

Salten Pt.

Salten Pt. Rd.

Rendezvous La.

START

Sturgis Library

6A

6

HOW to get there

Take 6A to Barnstable and watch for the Sturgis Library on your left, shortly after passing Rendezvous Road. Park in the library's parking lot.

No. 4 Barnstable–Cummaquid

and ride 0.5 mile to Yarmouth Port, to the intersection with Strawberry Lane on the right and Church Street on the left. Along this stretch are several attractions to visit briefly or to linger over. Three notable houses, which represent 300 years of New England architecture, are open to the public: the Colonel John Thatcher House (1680), the Winslow Crocker House (1780), and the Captain Bangs Hallet House (1840). The Botanical Trail commences at the Hallet House. The houses and trail are administered lovingly by the Historical Society of Old Yarmouth Port.

After enjoying Yarmouth Port, turn around and head west again on Route 6A. Turn right on Commerce Road, which circles a marsh and crosses Maraspin Creek. At Mill Way turn right for a short ride to the parking lot at Blish Point, overlooking Mill Way Beach and Barnstable Harbor—dotted with islands—sheltered by Sandy Neck across the way (which you may visit on Ride 3).

Retrace the route up Mill Way past the town docks to 6A. Turn right. Ride past the Sturgis Library (where your vehicle is parked), then turn right on Rendezvous Lane for another short jaunt to the water. On the way down to or back from the end of Rendezvous Lane (which dead-ends at the water, providing a good picnic site), turn into Salten Point Road. This road makes a loop and returns you to Rendezvous Lane. It offers some stunning glimpses of the harbor as well as a closer look at the lifestyle of some of Barnstable's burghers, whose well-appointed houses and lawns are on display around this circle. Return to 6A, turn left, and head back to the Sturgis Library, which is housed in the oldest building (1644) of any public library in the United States. Its collections, which date back to the seventeenth century, include a 1603 Bible, as well as extensive material relating to Cape Cod's history and genealogy.

The Trayser Memorial Museum is also located in Barnstable on 6A. It was originally a Customs House. An old jail building is on the grounds. The collection is open to the public for a modest charge Tuesday through Saturday from 1:00 to 5:00 P.M.

Woods Hole–Falmouth

Number of miles:	26.5
Approximate pedaling time:	3 hours
Terrain:	Varied—a lot of flat areas, other definitely hilly areas
Surface:	Good
Things to see:	Woods Hole Oceanographic Exhibit Center, Woods Hole Aquarium, views of Buzzard's Bay and Vineyard Sound, Falmouth Historical Society Museum, Spohr's Garden

Ride south on Route 28A and bear right onto Palmer Avenue at the flashing caution light. Go down Palmer to the bottom of the hill and turn right at the fork onto a very pretty, narrow country road called Sippewisset Road. Turn right on Beccles Road for a brief loop that returns you to Sippewisset Road. When you get to the crest of the hill, you'll see what formerly was the Cape Codder Hotel, now converted into condominiums, on the bluff to the right.

Upon leaving the crest, you'll be riding mainly downhill to Woods Hole. At the first stop sign, your route becomes Quisset Avenue; Oyster Pond Road will be on the left; however, the street sign may be missing. Turn left and go down Oyster Pond Road about 0.5 mile past Route 28A, which has double traffic lights, to Fells Road, where you make a sharp left onto Fells Road and ride a short distance to Spohr's Garden, on your right. This is truly a one-of-a-kind place: a private estate created by Mr. Spohr, an engineer, who has invited the public to view his lovely garden, situated on the shore of Oyster Pond. One of the unusual things about this beautiful place is that, as of the sum-

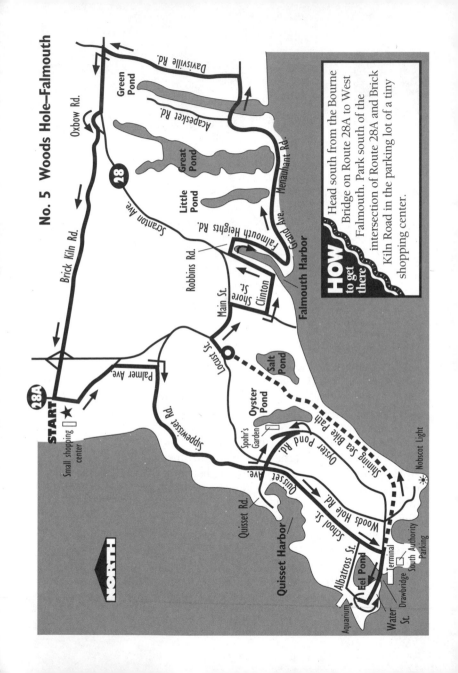

No. 5 Woods Hole–Falmouth

HOW to get there
Head south from the Bourne Bridge on Route 28A to West Falmouth. Park south of the intersection of Route 28A and Brick Kiln Road in the parking lot of a tiny shopping center.

NORTH

Brick Kiln Rd.

Oxbow Rd.

Davisville Rd.

Green Pond

Acapesket Rd.

28

Great Pond

Stanton Ave.

Little Pond

Menaunant Rd.

Grand Ave.

Falmouth Heights Rd.

Robbins Rd.

Main St.

Falmouth Harbor

Clinton St.

Shore St.

28A

START

Small shopping center

Palmer Ave.

Locust St.

Sippiwissett Rd.

Salt Pond

Spohr's Garden

Oyster Pond

Shining Sea Bike Path

Oyster Pond Rd.

Quisset Rd.

Quisset Ave.

Quisset Harbor

School St.

Woods Hole Rd.

Nobscot Light

Albatross St.

Eel Pond

Aquarium

Water St.

Drawbridge

Terminal

South Authority Parking

mer of 1996, it was not listed in any of the many informational publications about the Cape. An old and dear friend of mine who has a house about a mile away told me about it. In the garden there is also an extraordinary outdoor museum, which I will leave for you to discover for yourself. When you are ready to continue the ride, retrace your route back up to Quisset Avenue and turn left for a downhill run into the center of Woods Hole on what is now called School Street. Watch for a building on your left just before you come to the T with Water Street; it houses the Exhibit Center of the Woods Hole Oceanographic Institute and is well worth a visit.

Eel Pond is the crowded anchorage to your right as you come into town; the buildings bordering the pond are those of the three marine research institutions: the National Marine Fisheries Service, the Marine Biological Laboratory, and the Woods Hole Oceanographic Institute. Watch for the research vessels R/V *Albatross* and R/V *Dolphin*, and visit the Woods Hole Aquarium, which is run by the National Marine Fisheries Service and is free. Quisset Avenue—now School Street—comes to a T at Water Street. Go right on Water Street to the research facilities and to see the Candle House. A unique ship's bow sticks out of the front of the building.

To continue your route, come back on Water Street to the entrance to the Steamship Authority ferry landing. (The Steamship Authority Terminal has rest rooms!) Turn right and then left into the large parking lot through the pedestrian entrance. Once in the parking lot, turn to your left and ride to the end of the lot, under the overpass. Here you will find the Woods Hole end of the Shining Sea Bikeway, a traffic-free ride for 3.3 miles along Vineyard Sound to downtown Falmouth.

You'll emerge from the dramatic bikeway onto Locust Street. Bear right. At the fork bear right again onto West Main Street by the Falmouth Green. Watch for the elegant 1790 Colonial across the green, which is the Falmouth Historical Society Museum.

At Shore Street turn right and go down to the water, see the Town Beach, and then go back up Shore 2 blocks to Clinton and turn right. Ride about 5 blocks to Scranton Avenue on the Falmouth Inner Harbor. Skirt this beautiful, active harbor by going left on Scranton, right on Robbins Road at the top of the harbor, and right on Falmouth Heights Road to go down the east side. This is another site from which you can ferry to Martha's Vineyard.

Bear right at the fork onto Grand Avenue and turn sharply left as it skirts Vineyard Sound. Continue along this road, which becomes Menauhant Road, passing Little Pond and Great Pond. At the fork with Ocean Avenue (or Vineyard Street, as it may be named), turn left and go inland, staying on Menauhant Road. At its intersection with Emerson (on the left), bear right, staying on Menauhant. Cross Acapesket Road, cross the bridge over Green Pond, and then turn left on Davisville Road.

Turn left at the traffic light on East Falmouth Highway, which is also Route 28. In about 0.75 mile, cross the Coonamesett River and turn right on Oxbow Road. Curve around uphill and turn right, going uphill on Brick Kiln Road. Follow Brick Kiln for 3 miles to Route 28. Go under Route 28 to Route 28A and turn left to return to the shopping center parking lot.

Osterville–Centerville

Number of miles:	14
Approximate pedaling time:	1½ hours
Terrain:	Hilly
Surface:	Good
Things to see:	Towns of Osterville and Centerville; East, West, and Great bays; Crosby Yacht Yard; 1856 Country Store

Osterville and Centerville, two more of Barnstable's small villages, are side by side along Nantucket Sound on the southern shore of the Cape, and they will give you a close look at yet another side to the Cape Cod way of life.

You can start from the five-corner intersection of Main Street, Bay Street, Parker Road, Davis Lane, and again Main Street, parking your vehicle along Main. Head north on Main toward Falmouth. You'll pass Blossom Avenue and Emily Way, both on the right; when you come to Pond Street, turn right. Use the sidewalk on Pond and pass Tower Hill Road on the right. At the next street Pond Street becomes Bumps River Road, which comes in from the left. Continue straight on Bumps River Road.

Soon you will come to a fork in the road, just after Old Mill Road. Depending on the time of year, the street signs may be missing, having departed the scene with some larcenous visitor, so look for a green fire hydrant on the corner and bear right, continuing on Bumps River Road. If you continued straight ahead and then curved to the left, you would find that you were on Five Corners Road. At the T intersection turn left on what is Park Avenue, though once again it may not, alas, be so marked. Ride the short distance to Henry Place.

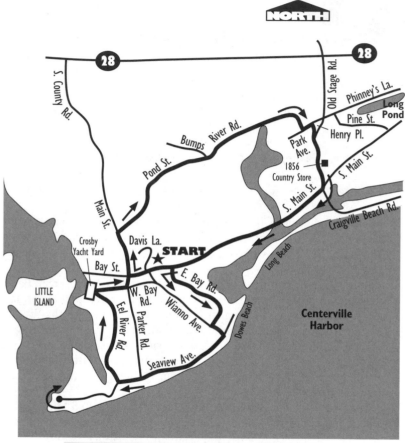

HOW to get there From the intersection of Routes 149 and 28, head east toward Hyannis on Route 28. Take South County Road to the right. It becomes Main Street and delivers you to the center of Osterville.

Turn right and immediately right again onto Main Street. Now you are in for a treat, as Centerville's Main Street is exceptional. There are stately old houses on both sides of the street, a handsome church, and the 1856 Country Store, which is stuffed with handmade crafts and enough gadgets to satisfy anyone.

Where Main Street intersects with South Main Street, there is a traffic light; turn right, following the sign to OSTERVILLE. Proceed on South Main Street and enjoy the views of East Bay. Turn left onto East Bay Road, following it to the T intersection with Wianno Avenue. Turn left and ride to Dowes Beach. Wianno Avenue comes to a T at Seaview Avenue; turn right and follow Seaview. After passing the gatehouses, backyards, and driveways of those that have deep pockets, you'll arrive at the end of Seaview Avenue. Here you'll be looking at a sandbar called Dead Neck, Grand Island, and West Bay.

After enjoying the scene, retrace your route to just past Eel River and turn left on Eel River Road. It will come to a T at West Bay Road. Turn left. Immediately you'll be at the Crosby Yacht Yard. Operational since 1840, this yard was the home of the Crosby Cat, the original Catboat. There are rest rooms here.

Leaving Crosby's, turn left on West Bay Road and then turn left on Parker Road—which turns into Main Street—and return to the village of Osterville. Before you leave the village, take a stroll along Main Street. You may find just the item you've been looking for, or a souvenir—or a snack at a little restaurant.

Hyannis

Number of miles:	13.5
Approximate pedaling time:	2 hours
Terrain:	Mostly flat, a few moderate hills
Surface:	Good
Things to see:	Hyannis Harbor, Sunset Hill, Craigville Beach, 1856 Country Store, Kalmus Park Beach, John F. Kennedy Memorial

Barnstable is the Cape's largest town, and Hyannis is its largest village, the "hub" of the Cape, attracting more visitors throughout the year than any other village. Hyannis is not as pleasing to the eye and the soul as the smaller, quainter villages but has much to offer the visitor: more accommodations, entertainment, shopping (the largest shopping center on the Cape is here, the Cape Cod Mall, on Route 132), and, of course, dining to suit every palate and wallet.

Begin the ride from the large parking lot for the Antique Co-op & Flea Market, at the corner of Main Street and High School Road in Hyannis. Turn right on Main, going west (it's one-way in this direction); use the sidewalk wherever possible, giving pedestrians the right-of-way. At Sea Street turn left and head south, passing bed-and-breakfast inns on both sides of the street as you head for the water. It's 1 mile to Ocean Avenue, where you bear right forty-five degrees to ride alongside the harbor and town beach for 0.5 mile to a T intersection with Hyannis Avenue. Turn left on Hyannis. Note the sign TOUR BUSES TURN RIGHT. The buses come to these short and narrow streets to show what they can of the Kennedy family compound of summer homes.

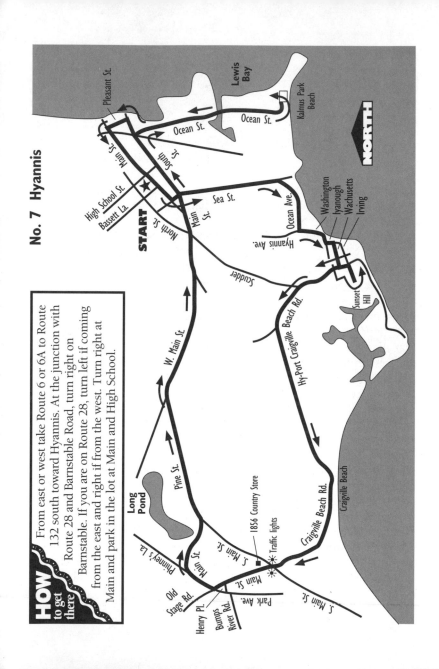

No. 7 Hyannis

HOW to get there

From east or west take Route 6 or 6A to Route 132 south toward Hyannis. At the junction with Route 28 and Barnstable Road, turn right on Barnstable. If you are on Route 28, turn left if coming from the east and right if from the west. Turn right at Main and park in the lot at Main and High School.

START

Pleasant St.

Lewis Bay

Ocean St.

Ocean St.

Kalmus Park Beach

NORTH

Main St.

South St.

High School St.

Bassett La.

Sea St.

Ocean Ave.

Washington
Iyanough
Wachusetts
Irving

North St.

Main St.

Hyannis Ave.

Scudder

Sunset Hill

W. Main St.

Hy-Port Craigville Beach Rd.

Long Pond

Pine St.

1856 Country Store

Traffic lights

Craigville Beach Rd.

Craigville Beach

Phinney's La.

Old Stage Rd.

Henry Pl.

Bumps River Rd.

Main St.

S. Main St.

Park Ave.

Main St.

S. Main St.

Hyannis Avenue quickly turns right almost ninety degrees and becomes Washington Avenue. Turn left at the first street, Iyanough, and immediately right onto Wachusetts Avenue. Turn left at the T intersection with Scudder, go 1 block, turn right onto Irving Avenue, and go up the short hill to the end of Irving. This is Sunset Hill, which used to be a public overlook where you could see the sunset and two of the Kennedy homes down on the shore. Because of the tragic history of the Kennedys, the overlook is now fenced off, owned by a private golf club. There is still a view; it's just not what it was. (In April 1996 the gate to the fence was wide open and the small stone church on the low hill to the right was boarded up. Let me know what you find.) When you are ready, go back to Scudder and turn left, riding downhill to the Y intersection with Hy-Port Craigville Beach Road. There's a firehouse on the right. Go left onto Hy-Port Craigville Beach Road, which curves left and then straightens out after it passes another Y, where it becomes Craigville Beach Road again. Keep to the left, past Strawberry Hill Road, until you reach crescent-shaped Craigville Beach, which, together with Covell and Downs beaches, forms the beaches of Craigville Harbor, a large portion of which is public and a lovely place to swim.

To continue, follow Craigville Beach Road as it curves right, going inland, over the Centerville River to a traffic light at the intersection of South Main Street on the right and left (and a sign reading OSTERVILLE) and your road, which goes across South Main Street and then becomes Main Street. Straight ahead is the 1856 Country Store, a must stop. On this remarkable street you'll pass one stately house after another, including the Mary Lincoln House (1840), now a museum of the Centerville Historical Society.

Just past the museum, a short street, Henry Place, comes in from the left, forming the base of the triangular intersection of Main Street, Park, and Old Stage Road. Bear right, continuing on Main, which quickly comes to another Y, this time with Phinney's Lane straight ahead. Bear right again, continuing on Main as it curves to the right around the south end of Long Pond to a stop sign, where Main merges into Pine Street coming in from the right. Continue on what is now Pine Street for about 0.75 mile to a stop sign at the T intersection with West Main Street. Turn right onto West Main and use the sidewalk. In about a mile you'll come to a traffic light at Pitchers Way. Continue across on West Main for 0.5 mile to a rotary, from which you go right on Main (after Scudder). Main soon forks; bear right onto South Street. If it's getting late or you are tired, you could turn left when you get to High School Road and ride the 1 block to your starting place. If you're still rarin' to go, ride about 7 blocks to Ocean Street, turn right, and ride down to the town park alongside Lewis Bay, where you can see lots of boat action: large ferries to the islands backing and turning, fishing trawlers, and private yachts—a cornucopia for boat watchers. And last but not least, you'll also find rest rooms (in summer only) and places to lock up your bike.

If you'd like a swim or a walk on a lovely beach, continue down Ocean about 0.5 mile to Kalmus Park Beach. When you are ready, return up Ocean to South Street. To avoid the heavy traffic here, turn right on South and ride the short distance to Pleasant, where you turn left and ride to Main Street; turn left and ride down to the starting place at High School Road and Main. Before you leave Hyannis, take a stroll up and down Main Street. You'll have lots of relaxed company as you browse the many stores and places for dining and entertainment.

West Yarmouth–
South Yarmouth

Number of miles:	14.5
Approximate pedaling time:	2 hours
Terrain:	Moderately hilly
Surface:	Good
Things to see:	Judah Baker Windmill, Yarmouth Herring Run

West and South Yarmouth, villages within the town of Yarmouth, lie along the southern shore of Yarmouth, on Nantucket Sound. The area along Route 28 is one of the most popular tourist centers on the Cape, because it has an abundance of family motels, family restaurants, shopping centers, places of amusement and entertainment, and the warm water beaches on Nantucket Sound.

You can start the ride by parking your vehicle in the Friendly's Restaurant parking lot on the northeast corner of Route 28 (Main Street) and Higgins Crowell Road in West Yarmouth. Go right (north) on Higgins Crowell Road. A sign will point to Route 6. Go through the typical Cape Cod pine forest here, uphill for 0.8 mile to the juncture with Buck Island Road; turn right. This is a well-paved two-lane road that goes by cranberry bogs, off to the right. Come to West Yarmouth Road. Turn left on this two-lane road. Pass through patches of open countryside, still climbing, as you go inland from the shore. Three miles into the ride, you come to Old Town House Road; turn right. There is a country feeling out here where the land is sparsely settled. Old Town House Road is a big three-lane road still going uphill. In 1.25 miles turn right on Station Avenue, a gently rolling road, which goes mostly downhill.

Just past the regional high school on your left, across the football

No. 8 Yarmouth–So. Yarmouth

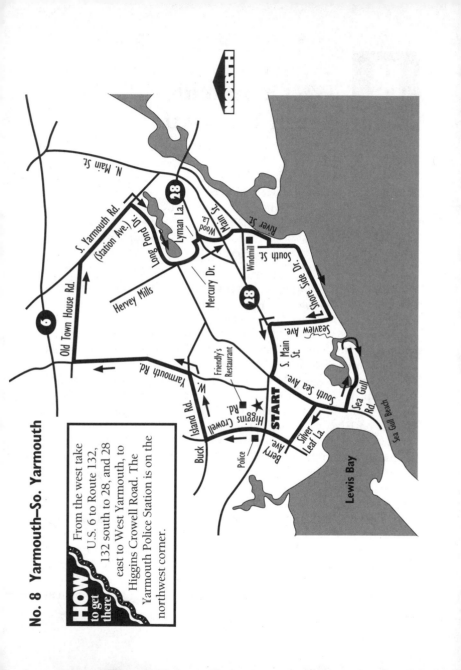

HOW to get there

From the west take U.S. 6 to Route 132, 132 south to 28, and 28 east to West Yarmouth, to Higgins Crowell Road. The Yarmouth Police Station is on the northwest corner.

NORTH

Old Town House Rd.

S. Yarmouth Rd. (Station Ave.)

N. Main St.

Long Pond Dr.

Lyman La.

28

Hervey Mills

Wood La.

Main St.

Mercury Dr.

Windmill

River St.

South St.

28

Shore Side Dr.

Seaview Ave.

Yarmouth Rd.

Friendly's Restaurant

S. Main St.

W. Higgins Crowell Rd.

Buck Island Rd.

START

Police

Berry Ave.

South Sea Ave.

Silver Leaf La.

Sea Gull Rd.

Sea Gull Beach

Lewis Bay

field, turn right onto Long Pond Drive. Skirt Long Pond, which you can glimpse through the trees to your left. At the end of Long Pond, after passing Winslow Gray Road on the right, turn left on Mercury Drive. At the point where Venus Road comes in from the right and Mars Lane also goes off at an angle to the right, continue straight ahead on Mercury Drive, which will T into Lyman Lane. Turn right on little Lyman Lane and go down to Route 28; turn left and then immediately right onto Wood Lane. Go past a small, wooded lane divider where there's a statue of a fireman. Just past this spot turn right onto Wood Road, a narrow residential street. Cross Main Street (Route 28); the road you're on is now called River Street, which takes you down to and briefly along the Bass River.

At the fork with Pleasant Street, bear right on River Street. Soon after the fork you will come to the Judah Baker Windmill, on the bank of Bass River in tiny Windmill Park. There's a nice little beach here. The windmill was originally built in 1791 in South Dennis and moved here in 1863. The town now owns it and is restoring it. Continue on River Street, which swings around ninety degrees to the right and then comes to South Street, where there's a stop sign. Turn left onto South Street, which takes you down to Shore Side Drive. Run Pond is on your right. Smuggler's or Bass River Beach is here on the curve just as you get to the shoreline. There are lots of motels, cottages, and quiet houses. You are now on Shore Side Drive. Proceed along the waterfront. There are houses between you and the water, but you can go down any one of the streets running off to your left to the shore. Several public beaches can be found along this road.

At the stop sign at Seaview Avenue, turn left past the Beach House Motor Lodge to the point, a nice place to take a break and get a great, unimpeded view of the ocean. Turn around and go straight up Seaview Avenue to Main Street (also Route 28). At the stop sign turn left. When you come to South Sea Avenue and a traffic light, turn left and return to the shoreline.

Sea Gull Road comes up in a mile; turn left onto it and head for Sea Gull Beach. Lewis Pond will be in sight to your left. Stretches of the road become a causeway across the marshes. Beautiful Sea Gull Beach is open from 8:00 A.M. to 10:00 P.M. There are rest room facilities (open in summer only). After your swim and/or picnic, return to South Sea Avenue via Sea Gull Road. Turn right on South Sea and then, about 4 blocks up, turn left onto Silver Leaf Lane, which will take you 0.6 mile to Berry Avenue. There is a stop sign, but there may not be a street sign; however, you'll be able to identify it because Silver Leaf Lane jogs to the left after it crosses Berry. Turn right on Berry, which will take you back up to South Main Street, where you started your ride.

West Dennis–Harwich Port

Number of miles:	18
Approximate pedaling time:	2 hours
Terrain:	Flat to moderately hilly
Surface:	Good
Things to see:	Towns of Harwich and Harwich Port, Cape Cod Rail Trail, Allen's Harbor, Glendon Beach, Swan River, West Dennis Beach

This ride will take you through interesting parts of West Dennis and Dennis Port, two of the five villages that constitute the town of Dennis, which stretches from one side of the Cape to the other and through equally interesting sections of two of Harwich's seven villages, Harwich Center and Harwich Port. You will also get a taste of the 20-mile Cape Cod Rail Trail for 4.5 miles: from its beginning at Route 134 in West Dennis to Route 124 to Harwich Center.

Start the ride in the parking lot of the Ezra H. Baker Public School, on the corner of Route 28 and Trotting Park Road. Leave the parking lot and turn right, heading north on Trotting Park Road. A stop sign comes up shortly at the intersection with Center Street. You should see a sign here that indicates OLD MAIN STREET to the left. You continue across and to the right forty-five degrees onto a paved, wide two-lane road. You'll pass Pine Field Lane and Lockwood Drive and a well-preserved old Congregational church. Bear left at the small island with an equally small stone marker, past a public library to the intersection with High Bank Road, also called Great Western Road. A building called Liberty Hall is on the opposite corner; turn right and go the short distance to the traffic light at Route 134. With great cau-

No. 9 West Dennis–Harwichport

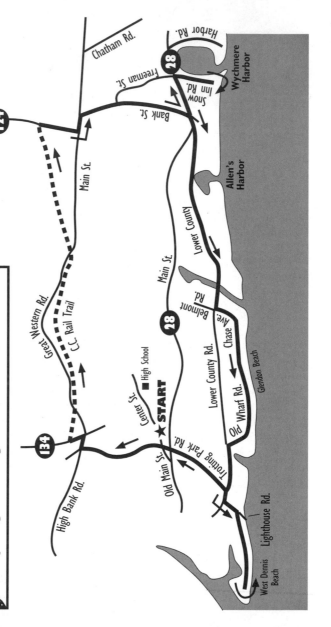

HOW to get there

From the west take Route 6 to Route 134 in South Dennis. Take 134 south to Route 28, turn right onto Route 28, and proceed 0.75 mile to the intersection of Route 28 and Trotting Park Road and the parking lot of the high school, on the northeast corner.

Chatham Rd.

Harbor Rd.

Wychmere Harbor

Freeman St.

Snow Inn Rd.

Bank St.

Allen's Harbor

Main St.

Lower County

Belmont Rd.

Main St.

Great Western Rd.

C.C. Rail Trail

Chase Ave.

Lower County Rd.

Glendon Beach

Center St.

■ High School

★ START

Old Wharf Rd.

High Bank Rd.

Old Main St.

Trotting Park Rd.

Lighthouse Rd.

West Dennis Beach

124

134

28

28

tion go straight across Route 134 and turn left onto a bike path on the right side of the road. Ride about 0.25 mile to the well-marked entrance to the Cape Cod Rail Trail. You now will have a 4.5-mile, traffic-free ride all the way to Route 124. When you reach 124, turn off the trail and ride down 124 approximately 1 mile to Main Street in Harwich; turn left on Main.

Riding along on Main Street, watch for Bank Street as you enjoy Harwich Center, which is a picturesque village with old houses and a pleasant air.

Leaving Harwich Center on Bank Street, you'll have a good down-hill run to Harwich Port past cranberry bogs on both sides, for a nice 1.5-mile ride. At the junction of Route 28 and Bank Street, turn right and ride west on 28 until the fork where Route 28 goes off to the right and Lower County Road bears left. (If you have time, take a de-tour down to Wychmere Harbor by turning left when Bank Street comes to a T at Route 28 and going east for about 0.25 mile to Snow Inn Harbor Road. Turn right. Ride down Snow Inn Road, to a white balcony that overlooks the harbor. It is just before the private club on the left, formerly the Thompson Clam Bar. From here you'll have a view of one of the loveliest of the small harbors the Cape is famous for.)

When you return to Route 28, you will take Lower County Road, to the left at the fork, and ride through Harwich Port with its old houses, churches, and little shops. Continue past Allen's Harbor, a tiny protected harbor right off the road, and over the Herring River into Dennis Port, where you'll see some of the southernmost part of that town. There is a lovely view of the harbor, the docks, and the windmill out on the point.

Turn left on Belmont Road and at the end of it turn right on Chase Avenue where the road parallels Motel Mecca. Follow closely when it goes right and then turn immediately left onto Old Wharf Road. At the five-way intersection, cross Sea Street and continue straight ahead on Old Wharf Road; you'll come upon Glendon Beach, which is public. Old Wharf Road ends at the stop sign at Lower County Road; turn left.

Shortly afterward cross over the Swan River with its fascinating marshlands. Turn left onto Lighthouse Road. There will be a sign to the Town Beach right across from a marsh; continue down to the extensive and beautiful West Dennis Public Beach. When you're ready to go, return up Lighthouse Road to Lower County Road and turn right. Ride as far as Trotting Park Road; turn left. Ride 1 mile back to your starting place at Route 28 and Trotting Park Road.

Harwich Center–
West Chatham

Number of miles:	13
Approximate pedaling time:	2 hours
Terrain:	Rolling hills
Surface:	Good
Things to see:	Village of Harwich Center, Brooks Free Library, town beach, Ridgevale Beach, central Cape Cod countryside

In this ride we begin with a closer look at Harwich Center with its graceful white Congregational church and a Main Street lined with antiques shops, one of the few types of stores that *expect* people to browse.

Start your ride on Main Street, near the junction of Routes 39 and 124. If you have pannier bags, you might find yourself stopping to purchase that small geegaw you've looked for everywhere.

Ride east on Main Street, past the Brooks Free Library. You might stop in here to see the collection of nineteenth-century statuary by John Roger. The statues are set in a Victorian atmosphere. Then you pass the bandstand and ball field to a Y, where you will bear right on Chatham Road. Main Street is lined with trees that are larger and taller than those found closer to the sea. One and a half miles down Chatham Road, you'll come to a T intersection with Route 28. Turn right on 28 and ride a short distance to Deep Hole Road; turn left and ride 0.5 mile down to the small but lovely town beach. There are rest rooms here. When you're ready to leave, take the road that starts just across from the rest rooms (open in summer only). This is Uncle Venies Road, although it may not be so marked.

Ride up 0.25 mile and turn right onto South Chatham Road. The

No. 10 Harwich Center–West Chatham

HOW to get there

From the west take Route 6 to Route 124 in the town of Harwich. Go right on 124 to the intersection of 124, Main Street, and Route 39 (Sisson Road). From the east turn left on 124.

NORTH

WEST CHATHAM

HARWICH

SOUTH HARWICH

★ START

Town Beach

Cockle Cove Rd.

Sam Ryders Rd.

Church St.

Old Queen Anne Rd.

Morton Rd.

Long Pond Rd.

Queen Anne Rd.

John Joseph Rd.

Depot Rd.

Pleasant St.

Main St.

Deep Hole Rd.

Uncle Venies Rd.

Deep Hole Rd.

Chatham Rd.

Orleans-Harwich Rd.

Oak St.

Bank St.

Main St.

137

39

39

124

28

137

28

route is parallel to the beach and ocean here and provides a fine view across the salt marsh. Pass Soundview, coming in from the left. Once you pass over into West Chatham, this road becomes Deep Hole Road, although there might not be a sign. The road goes uphill for a short distance and then levels off just before the T intersection with Pleasant Street. There's a stop sign here. Turn left onto Pleasant Street and ride up to Route 28. Turn right onto 28, where you'll see a village store and snack bar on the corner. This is a rolling road. Follow it past Route 137, which comes in from the left, to Sam Ryders Road; turn left.

It's mostly uphill here for almost 1 mile to a T intersection with Queen Anne Road. Turn left here. Stay on Queen Anne Road for 4 miles, to the intersection with Route 124. Queen Anne Road is not well marked, so follow the map and instructions carefully. Pass Church Street and then cross Route 137, which bends here and is called Morton Road on your left and Long Pond on your right. Continue straight, and soon Cemetery Road will come in from your right and merge into Queen Anne Road. Stay on Queen Anne. You'll come to a stop sign on Route 39; cross over and continue past a small pond, and then Bucks Pond and Josephs Pond, all on your left. Just past the ponds the road widens. At the intersection of Queen Anne Road and Route 124, there is a stop sign. Turn left onto Route 124, which is called Pleasant Lake Road. From here the route is mostly downhill for 1 mile to Harwich Center and your starting place.

The Cape Cod Rail Trail

Number of miles:	25 one way
Approximate pedaling time:	3½ to 6 hours
Terrain:	Flat to moderately hilly
Surface:	Excellent
Things to see:	Freshwater lakes (called ponds), forests, saltwater and freshwater marshes, cranberry bogs, Rock Harbor and all the flora and fauna contained therein, Salt Pond Visitor Center

This unique ride is off the road, on its own 8-foot-wide bicycle "street," for 23 of its total length of 25 miles. Except for a short distance on West Road in Orleans to pass over Route 6 and for 2.1 miles on Main Street and Rock Harbor Road, also in Orleans, it runs along the abandoned right-of-way of the old Penn Central Railroad from Route 134 in South Dennis to Locust Road in Eastham, the former terminus. A new 5-mile extension runs from Locust Road to a tunnel under Route 6, then ninety degrees left, straight up to Lecount Hollow Road. This section of the trail is out in the open; consequently, it's rather dull but with perhaps a saving grace of providing rest stops along the way where one can meet and chat with fellow bicyclists from many parts of the country.

Since there are parking lots at each end of the trail, as well as at Route 124 in Harwich and Nickerson State Park in Brewster, you could begin your ride at any one of these points. Rest areas and rest rooms can be found at the Dennis Town Hall just west of the Route 134 terminus, on Old Bass River Road, at Nickerson State Park, at the Salt Pond Visitor Center, and at most town beaches.

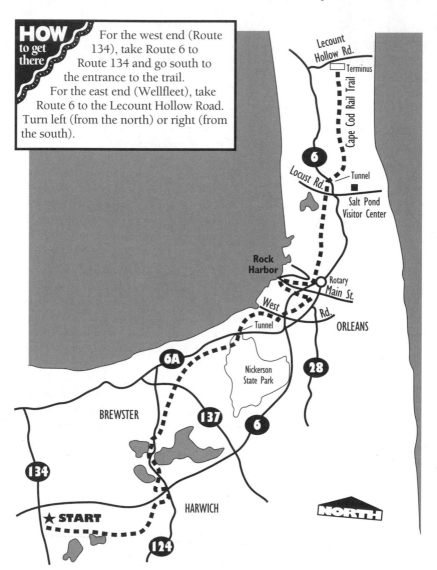

HOW to get there

For the west end (Route 134), take Route 6 to Route 134 and go south to the entrance to the trail.

For the east end (Wellfleet), take Route 6 to the Lecount Hollow Road. Turn left (from the north) or right (from the south).

Lecount Hollow Rd.

Terminus

Cape Cod Rail Trail

Locust Rd.

Tunnel

Salt Pond Visitor Center

Rock Harbor

Rotary
Main St.

West

Rd.

ORLEANS

Tunnel

Nickerson State Park

BREWSTER

NORTH

★ START

HARWICH

If you decide to start at the Route 134 end, as you travel along the trail you will pass many freshwater ponds, created thousands of years ago by tremendous blocks of ice left behind by the retreating glacier. Sand Pond, Hinkley's Pond, Seymour, and Long Pond are a few of these "kettle" ponds you will pass. At the intersection with Route 6A in Brewster, you will come alongside Nickerson State Park, 2,000 acres, with four ponds ranging in size from 18 to 204 acres, more than 400 campsites, and 8 miles of bike paths. Just past the park the trail will go under Route 6A through its own small tunnel and enter the area of salt marshes such as the Namskaket Creek, a classic example of a barrier beach salt marsh system, which will be on your left. After this, when the trail reaches Orleans, it will take you out onto Main Street, where you turn left and ride through the Orleans business district, with shops of all kinds (plus motorized vehicles—so be alert!). It's a short detour down to Rock Harbor, a small fishing harbor with a beach for swimming. When you leave this neat place, turn left (a left-hand turn facing inland), paralleling Route 6. The bike trail soon reappears on the left side of the road. Farther north the freshwater ponds reappear, and the ride comes to Locust Road in Eastham, 0.25 mile from the Salt Pond Visitor Center on Route 6. This beautiful facility of the Cape Cod National Seashore blends artistically into the landscape and through its exhibits and films provides a fascinating glimpse into the human and natural history of the Cape—plus giving you a breathtaking view of a tremendous salt pond. If you haven't been in this visitor center before, don't miss it now. Besides its main facilities, it has a fine 2-mile bike trail, the Nauset Marsh Trail, that takes you up to and down from Coast Guard Beach and Station. (There's a description of Nauset Marsh Trail in Ride 16.)

I think the best way to ride the Cape Cod Rail Trail is to do it over a three-day period: from Route 134 to Nickerson State Park and back (or the reverse) on one day, from Nickerson State Park to the Salt Pond Visitor Center and back (or the reverse) on another day, and from the Visitor Center to the northern end at Lecount Hollow Road and back on the third.

West Brewster–Dennis

Number of miles:	21
Approximate pedaling time:	3 hours
Terrain:	Hilly
Surface:	Good to excellent
Things to see:	Stony Brook Grist Mill, Chapin Beach, New England Fire and History Museum, Sesuit Neck Harbor, Museum of Natural History and Josiah Dennis Manse, Scargo Observation Tower, Scargo Lake

Brewster and Dennis are side by side along Cape Cod Sound on the northern coastline of the Cape, and both were home to many a seagoing captain when he wasn't sailing the seven seas back in the early nineteenth century. To captain an oceangoing sailing vessel took an extraordinary man, and because so many of these men lived in Brewster, it was called "The Sea Captain Town." There are three museums at various places on the ride. Visit all of them—especially the New England Fire and History Museum, at your starting place—to get the full flavor of the history of this part of the Cape.

Begin the ride on Route 6A just west of Route 137 (Long Pond Road). Park in the lot of the New England Fire and History Museum. Come out of the parking lot and turn right onto Main Street (Route 6A). At the fork where 6A goes right, take the left-hand one, which is Stony Brook Road. There's also a sign indicating a bike route in this direction. You'll pass Smith Pond on the left and then a series of ponds.

You'll soon begin a stiff uphill and then take a steep downhill.

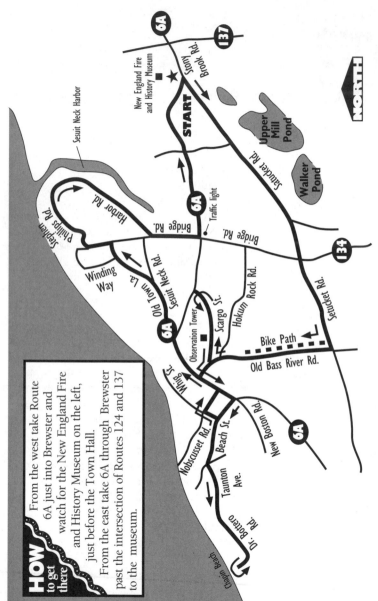

HOW to get there

From the west take Route 6A just into Brewster and watch for the New England Fire and History Museum on the left, just before the Town Hall.

From the east take 6A through Brewster past the intersection of Routes 124 and 137 to the museum.

New England Fire and History Museum

Sesuit Neck Harbor

Stephen Phillips Rd.

Harbor Rd.

Winding Way

Old Town La.

Sesuit Neck Rd.

Observation Tower

Scargo St.

Hokum Rock Rd.

Bike Path

Old Bass River Rd.

Setucket Rd.

Wing St.

Nobscusset Rd.

Beach St.

New Boston Rd.

Taunton Ave.

Dr. Bottero Rd.

Chapin Beach

START

Stony Brook Rd.

Sauder Rd.

Upper Mill Pond

Walker Pond

Bridge Rd.

Traffic light

6A

6A

6A

6A

6A

137

134

NORTH

No. 12 West Brewster–Dennis

About 0.75 mile from the fork, you'll come upon the Stony Brook Grist Mill on the left. This gristmill still works and demonstrations are given from 2:00 to 5:00 P.M. on Wednesday, Friday, and Saturday in July and August.

There is a fork just beyond the mill; here bear left onto Satucket Road—after a couple of miles, the road changes its name to Setucket. *Sa* or *Se*, it's still a hilly road. You pass a lovely, placid little pond and go through a forested area. Two miles from the fork of Satucket and Stony Brook roads, there is another pond, where you bear right, remaining on Satucket Road. There is much open, unsettled country here, very much like parts of Connecticut. In another mile cross Route 134. A half-mile after 134 you'll come to Old Bass River Road, which has a paved bike path alongside it. Turn right onto the bike path on the right side, and ride the 1.8 miles to Route 6A. The bike path ends about 0.5 mile from 6A. It is downhill here, and Hokum Rock Road and Scargo Road come sweeping in from your right, so exercise lots of caution while you make a sharp right-hand turn onto and up Scargo Road, a very steep hill. You may have to walk your bike, as the hill is 160 feet high, but at the top you'll find the Scargo Hill Observation Tower, from which you'll get a great view of both sides of the Cape—as much as 80 miles on a clear day. Tobey Memorial Park and Scargo Lake are also at the summit. The lake, formed by a glacier, is very deep and surrounded by pine trees.

The ride down will be the opposite from the one going up! Check your brakes and come on down. Be especially cautious as you enter Old Bass River Road on the way to Route 6A. Once at 6A, turn left, using the sidewalk, and go about 0.25 mile to where Route 6A makes a hard left and where you go right onto New Boston Road—just after Nobscusset Road and across from the Dennis Public Market. Almost immediately there is a fork with Beach Street; bear right onto Beach. East Bay View Street comes in from the right; you go left, heading for Chapin Beach, taking the farthest left road at the three-way fork, which is Taunton Avenue. Taunton soon turns right and then left, and here you will see a sign telling you that this little piece of road is Dr. Bottero Road. This is a dune-and-grass area with water on both sides. Continue out through the dunes. Just follow the paved road for as far as it goes and you'll come to Chapin Beach. It's on the bay side of the Cape, so the dunes and waves are smaller but still beautiful.

Return the way you came to Beach Street. Stay on Beach as far as Whig Street on the left. It's the next street after Tory Lane, *bien entendu!* Turn left onto Whig and go to the next intersection, with Nobscusset Road, and turn right. At the corner is the Josiah Dennis Manse, a gray-shingled house built in 1736 for Dennis. Did you know that *manse* means the residence of a minister?

Follow Nobscusset Road back to Route 6A, and then turn left and head east toward East Dennis and Brewster. Ride along 6A, using the sidewalks where available, for slightly more than a mile to the fork with Sesuit Neck Road. You go left onto Sesuit Neck Road while Route 6A goes right without you. Go down Sesuit Neck for about 0.5 mile until Old Town Lane comes in from the left. Turn left onto Old Town Lane and follow it to a charming little Y intersection with a tiny island and a vertical marker that indicates a road called Winding Way coming in from about ninety degrees left and Old Town Lane proceeding straight. You continue on Old Town Lane until it tees with Bridge Road, whereupon you turn left and, after a short distance, right onto Stephen Phillips Road. Follow Stephen Phillips as it turns left, down to the seashore and right on Harbor Road to Sesuit Neck Harbor. If the weather is fine, the land- and seascapes should make this tortuous route worthwhile. Continue around the busy little harbor on Harbor Road until it joins with and becomes Sesuit Neck Road. Continue until the intersection with Bridge Road, where you turn left and go up to Route 6A. Turn left on 6A and ride past the salt marshes into Brewster.

At the intersection where Stony Brook Road goes off to the right, go left. You will be on Main Street, Brewster, as well as Route 6A, and you'll soon come to the starting place at the New England Fire and History Museum.

Brewster–
Nickerson State Park

Number of miles:	16
Approximate pedaling time:	2½ hours
Terrain:	Moderately hilly
Surface:	Good
Things to see:	Nickerson State Park, Brewster,
	Brewster, and Harwich countryside

The 2,000 acres of Nickerson State Park, where the ride begins and ends, were donated by Addie Nickerson in 1934, in memory of her son, who died in 1918. Addie was the widow of Roland Nickerson, who owned the vast estate that these 2,000 acres were but a small part of—a village unto itself, extending to Cape Cod Sound, where there still exists the grand mansion of the estate, built in 1908, now the Ocean Edge resort and conference center. The Park itself has approximately eight miles of bike trails you can explore, if you've a mind to, either before you take off on this ride or when you return. A map of all the Park's trails can be obtained at the Park headquarters just inside the main entrance.

Start the ride in Nickerson State Park just off Route 6A in Brewster. In the summertime the parking lot just inside the entrance to the park is a holding area for campers. After Labor Day you can park here, but in the summer either park in the parking lot located 1,000 feet west of the entrance, off Route 6A, or go into the park a short distance straight ahead, just past the amphitheater, where there is a parking area on your right.

You can begin the ride here and start off on the bike path to the right. This paved path is just for you, and it winds its way mostly downhill for approximately 2 miles through the park.

No. 13 Brewster–Nickerson State Park

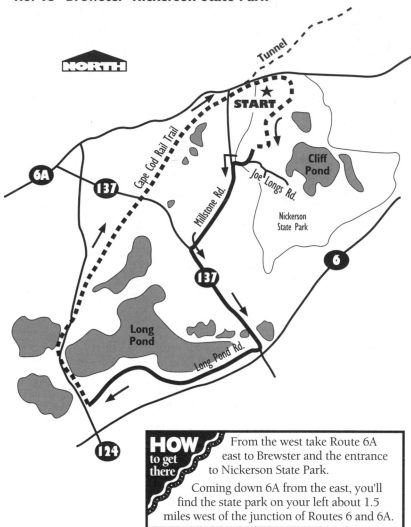

NORTH

Tunnel

★ **START**

Cape Cod Rail Trail

6A

137

Millstone Rd.

Joe Longs Rd.

Cliff Pond

137

Nickerson State Park

6

Long Pond

Long Pond Rd.

124

HOW to get there — From the west take Route 6A east to Brewster and the entrance to Nickerson State Park.

Coming down 6A from the east, you'll find the state park on your left about 1.5 miles west of the junction of Routes 6 and 6A.

Just after you pass the dumping station and the fire tower (off to your left), stay on the bike path as it turns right ninety degrees at an intersection of the park road (which turns left) and three other roads, all of which are outside the park. Access to these by car is barred by a gate. There are several private homes here on Windswept Road and Joe Longs Road. Here the bike path parallels Joe Longs Road. In 0.25 mile leave the park bike path and cross over to Joe Longs Road just before it comes to a **T** at Millstone Road, and then turn left onto Millstone Road. Ride on Millstone for about 1.5 miles until it tees into Route 137, which is also called Long Pond Road. Turn left and ride 2.5 miles through a forest where the colors are gorgeous in the fall, to the point, just before Route 6, where Long Pond Road goes right ninety degrees. Turn right and ride through scrub pine forests on either side. There will be an occasional glimpse of Long Pond on the right. When Long Pond tees into Route 124, turn right and get on the Cape Cod Rail Trail, which runs along Route 124 here. Take this marvelous bike path north for approximately 5.5 miles as it crisscrosses Route 124 by Long Pond and Seymour Pond and proceeds off to the north through the woods, past the Brewster Golf Club, right up to where it borders the waiting areas in Nickerson State Park. Here you turn right at the small sign NICKERSON STATE PARK and ride the very short distance on this spur of the Cape Cod Rail Trail into the park and return to your starting place. Just after this point the Rail Trail goes left and under Route 6A, so if you find yourself doing that, you have gone too far.

Chatham

Number of miles:	16
Approximate pedaling time:	2½ hours
Terrain:	Hilly to flat
Surface:	Good
Things to see:	The beautiful town and harbors of Chatham, Chatham Fish Pier, Chatham Lighthouse, Chatham Airport

Chatham is the elbow of the bent arm that Massachusetts thrusts out into the ocean. With water on three sides, Chatham is a village of narrow streets and cedar-shingled, sturdy homes lived in by innumerable generations, a place where Main Street is lined with antiques shops, crafts stores, and friendly coffee shops, and where fishermen still ply their dangerous calling by going out to sea in their small boats. It's a traditional town, casual and fun but refined—a delight! Cape Cod at its best.

Begin the ride in the parking lot of the shopping center at the junction of Queen Anne Road, Crowell Road, and Route 28 in Chatham. When you leave the parking lot bearing right on Queen Anne Road, you'll be on a marked bike route. At the Y continue right on Pond Street (Queen Anne Road goes up to the left). Circle enormous Oyster Pond, which has a public beach. At the stop sign of the T intersection, turn right onto Stage Harbor Road. At the Y intersection with Cedar Street, turn right onto Cedar Street. When Cedar Street comes to a T at Battlefield Road, turn left and ride along Battlefield until the intersection with Champlain Road. Turn left onto Champlain, still following the bike route. Very soon Champlain makes a ninety-degree bend to the left at the shore of Stage Harbor.

No. 14 Chatham

HOW to get there
From the west or east, take Route 28 directly into Chatham and proceed to the A&P at the intersection of Route 28, Crowell Road, Queen Anne Road, Depot Road, and Main Street.

28 Orleans Rd.

Scatteree Rd.

Stony Hill Rd.

Old Harbor Rd.

Queen Anne Rd.

Earl's Way

Crowell Rd.

Stepping Stone Rd.

Crowell Rd.

Stony Hill Rd.

28

TERN I.

George Ryders Rd.

Wilfred Rd.

Depot Rd.

28

Chatham Fish Pier

28

Chatham Airport

Main St.

Queen Anne Rd.

Pond St.

★ START

A&P ■

Oyster Pond

Seaview St.

Main St.

Shore Rd. Blvd.

Main St.

Barn Hill Rd.

Cedar St.

Stage Harbor Rd.

Chatham Lighthouse ■

Mill Pond

Hardings Beach Rd.

Battlefield Rd.

Champlain Rd.

Bridge St.

Hardings Beach

Morris Island Rd.

Monomoy Wildlife Refuge Headquarters ■

NORTH

You can see Stage Harbor Lighthouse out there as your route takes you along the shore of this beautiful harbor. Look for the nun and can buoys marking the channel. There are fishing boats at Old Mill Boatyard.

Champlain Road turns left and becomes Stage Harbor Road. Bear left, and shortly you will come to a stop sign where Bridge Street is on the right; turn right onto it. There's a nice little dock here. Go over the drawbridge and go straight until you come to a T with Morris Island Road. Turn right to go down Morris Island Road. On the left is the Chatham Lighthouse. When you come to Little Beach Road straight ahead, you bear right, continuing on Morris Island Road. Bear left and down and across the causeway. You're on Morris Island, and when you come to the end of the road you'll see a sign saying MONOMOY WILDLIFE REFUGE. The refuge headquarters is located on Morris Island, while most of the 2,750-acre refuge is located on the Monomoy Islands, accessible only by boat. When you're ready, double back across the causeway. At the stop sign continue straight past the Chatham Lighthouse on what is actually Main Street.

Take in the view, looking past Nauset Beach to the Atlantic. Main Street will curve up to the left. There may not be a street sign. There is a stop sign across from you and one for traffic coming down from your left but none on your side. Turn left, uphill—then dismount, lock up your bike, and walk! This little street of shops and happy, relaxed people is too lovely to pass on by. When you reach the spot where Seaview Street goes off to the right, if you have seen enough mount up again and turn sharply right onto Seaview and go up an incline so steep that you can get off and walk with impunity. Continue up and to the right to Shore Road, where you turn left, ride 1 long block, and turn sharply right at the sign TOWN OF CHATHAM FISH PIER. The professional fishing boats come in to this pier to unload their catch and they move fast, for time is of the essence! The fish have to be cleaned and iced down quickly. It's a rare sight for us landlubbers and one hard to pull oneself away from.

When you have pulled yourself away, go back to Shore Road and turn right. At the traffic light Old Harbor Road crosses Shore. Turn right onto Old Harbor Road and go downhill. At the T of Old Harbor and Scatteree roads, turn left on Scatteree, again following the bike route. Bend around to the left, downhill past Old Mail Road, on what is now called Stony Hill Road for about 0.6 mile until you come to Route 28, which is also Orleans Road. There may not be a sign, but it does look like a Route 28, what with a stop sign to hold you back and a Citgo station across the street on your left, so continue straight across Route 28 on Stony Hill Road, which will change its name to Stepping Stones Road after you pass Crowell Road. Next you will come to a five-corner intersection where little Earl's Way comes in at an angle from the right, Queen Anne Road comes across from the right and continues on to your left, and Stepping Stones continues straight as Wilfred Road. You turn right onto Queen Anne Road.

When George Ryders Road comes in from the left, turn left onto it and follow it to Chatham Airport, which has a restaurant and rest rooms. Continue on George Ryders Road a short distance to Route 28, where you turn left and, in about 0.25 mile, come to Barn Hill Road. It should be the second road after your turn onto Route 28. Turn right. This road goes downhill and curves left and right to a Y with Hardings Beach Road. Turn right on Hardings Beach Road and follow it to the beach. This is a public beach with sand dunes and rest rooms. Retrace the route back to Route 28, where you turn right and head back to your starting place via the bike path/sidewalk.

Orleans

Number of miles: 13
Approximate pedaling time: 2 hours
Terrain: Moderately hilly
Surface: Good
Things to see: French Cable Museum, Town Cove, Nauset Harbor, Nauset Beach, Rock Harbor

Orleans, so the story goes, was named for Louis-Philippe de Bourbon, Duc d'Orleans, who allegedly came to the area after his flight from France in the 1790s. Another French connection was the laying of a transatlantic communications cable by the Compagnie Francise des Cables Telegraphiques from Brest, France, to Orleans, completed in 1898. Today it is a lovely town—as you shall soon see—and the retailing and commercial center for this part of the Cape. Orleans offers you Nauset Beach, one of the Cape's finest, which goes on for miles along the Atlantic Ocean. Orleans also has Skaket Beach for swimming on Cape Cod Bay, where the water is warmer.

Start your ride in the Stop & Shop parking lot, which is across from the large Orleans Inn on Routes 6A and 28, just before the Orleans-Eastham town line. Leave your bike carrier here and ride out to 6A and 28; turn right. You quickly come to a Y intersection where 28 and 6A split. Bear left on Route 28. In 0.3 mile you come to Cove Road; turn left and go down the short hill to the shores of Town Cove. The tiny Orleans Yacht Club is located here at the innermost end of this long cove, which is bordered by Orleans and Eastham. Come back up the short but steep hill. You will be turning left here, but first take a look into the French Cable Museum on the corner. The building housed the U.S. terminus of the original Atlantic cable

No. 15 Orleans

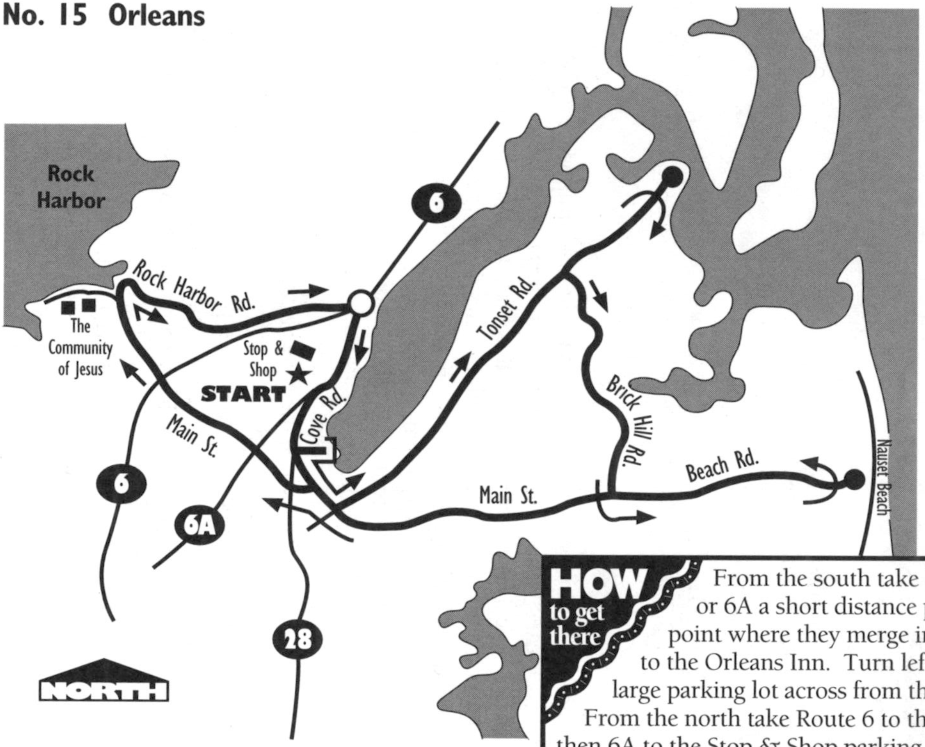

NORTH

Rock Harbor

The Community of Jesus

Rock Harbor Rd.

Stop & Shop
★
START

Main St.

6

6A

28

Cove Rd.

Main St.

6

Tonset Rd.

Brick Hill Rd.

Beach Rd.

Nauset Beach

HOW to get there

From the south take Route 28 or 6A a short distance past the point where they merge in Orleans to the Orleans Inn. Turn left into the large parking lot across from the inn. From the north take Route 6 to the rotary, then 6A to the Stop & Shop parking lot.

and is now a museum, open only Tuesday through Saturday in July and August, 2:00 to 4:00 P.M.

Now turn left onto 28 and ride to Main Street, where you turn ninety degrees left, on your way to Nauset Beach. Another short ride brings you to the intersection of Main Street and Tonset Road. Turn left onto Tonset. Over on your left there is a nice view of Town Cove. Continue on Tonset past woods on the left and characteristic Cape Cod houses on the right, past Gibson Road and Brick Hill Road, straight out to the dead end where Tonset Road overlooks Nauset Harbor, which is a cut through Nauset Beach. This is 3.5 miles from your starting point.

Turn around and go back up Tonset Road to Brick Hill Road and turn left. Continue on Brick Hill as it twists and turns, passing by Champlain and Tanglewood Terrace on your left. Soon after you pass Tanglewood, Brick Hill turns ninety degrees left and you turn with it. If you continued straight ahead, you'd be on Hopkins Lane. Your route takes you through wooded areas that are alive with color in the fall. About 1.5 miles from your turn onto Brick Hill, there is a T intersection with Beach Road. Unfortunately, you may not see a street sign here, but it is Beach Road, so turn left; in 0.6 mile, over to your right, you will feast your eyes on a stunning vista of the salt marshes with the beach in the distance.

From here to the beach, it is downhill; once there you will find a large parking lot, dressing rooms, rest rooms, a telephone, and a small refreshment stand, plus one gorgeous beach where you can swim, picnic, and/or walk in the dunes. Come back up the hill, retracing your route. Pass the intersection with Brick Hill Road and continue straight on Beach Road, passing the Barley Neck Inn and then, at a Y intersection with Main Street, bear to the right onto Main.

You'll pass the Orleans Theater and come to a stoplight at the intersection of Main and Tonset. Continue on Main Street, crossing Route 28 and then 6A. You are passing through the Orleans business district, with shops of all kinds, as you head toward the bay side and Rock Harbor, a tiny, bustling harbor, chock-full of fishing boats for professional fishermen and for amateurs. It's a very businesslike place with a restaurant and convenient dockside parking lot, plus an unusual surprise for you. When you turn your gaze from the water side of the parking lot, you will see something on the other side that you probably would not have expected to see in this setting: a large estate that houses a religious community called The Community of Jesus. There are close to 300 people living in the community, and they invite the public to join them for—as they put it—"the sort of summer activities that were once favorite New England pastimes—outdoor band concerts and barbecues, a church festival, Friday afternoon teas, a Sunday worship (in the Episcopal rite), and on Saturday afternoon, choral evensong. All are welcome, so come alone or bring a friend to this place of serenity overlooking Cape Cod Bay." Every Saturday, from July 10 through August 7, their sixty-five-piece "Spirit of America Concert Band" performs under a big tent on their grounds there in Rock Harbor at 7:30 P.M., after a buffet supper at 6:30.

When you are ready to continue, take Rock Harbor Road around to the left—a left-hand turn facing inland—and you'll soon find yourself paralleling Route 6. You will also pass a section of the off-road Cape Cod Rail Trail that begins again off to your left. Just past the Eastham-Orleans town line, turn right at the rotary onto Route 6A. Just before the traffic light at the entrance to the shopping center parking lot, you'll see a road on your right that will take you there, avoiding the traffic at the light.

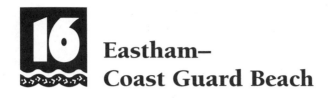

16 Eastham– Coast Guard Beach

Number of miles:	9.7
Approximate pedaling time:	1½ hours
Terrain:	Moderately hilly
Surface:	Good
Things to see:	Salt Pond Visitor Center, Eastham Historical Society Museum, Eastham Windmill, Great Pond, Nauset Light Beach, Coast Guard Beach

There are two visitors' centers in the National Park Service's Cape Cod National Seashore, and both are handsomely designed and architecturally well integrated with the landscape. Not only do they provide you with fascinating information about the human and natural history of the surrounding area through exhibits and illustrated orientation programs, but situated as they are on high ground, they also afford marvelous vistas of the seashore.

The Salt Pond Visitor Center overlooks the beautiful landscape of an enormous salt pond. Plan to spend at least several hours at the center upon your return and be sure to explore a bit of the Braille Nature Trail before you leave the parking lot. Proceed toward Route 6, past the Eastham Historical Society Museum on the right. It's open Wednesday and Friday afternoons in July and August.

Cross over Route 6 at the light and continue straight ahead on Locust Road to the Cape Cod Rail Trail on the left. Turn left and ride along the straight bike path for about 0.5 mile until you come to the first crossing, Samoset Road. Turn left and go up the short distance to the Eastham Windmill, which is in the small, triangular-shaped park. It still works! Turn around and come back down Samoset Road, past the Cape Cod Rail Trail to Great Pond Road, where you turn right. If

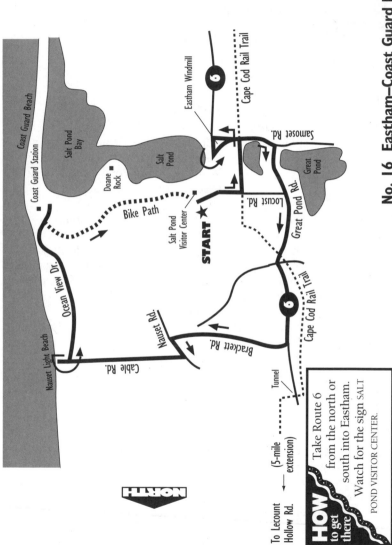

NORTH

Coast Guard Beach

Coast Guard Station

Salt Pond Bay

Doane Rock

Salt Pond

Eastham Windmill

Cape Cod Rail Trail

6

Samoset Rd.

Great Pond

Bike Path

Locust Rd.

Great Pond Rd.

Ocean View Dr.

Salt Pond Visitor Center

★ START

Nauset Light Beach

Nauset Rd.

Cape Cod Rail Trail

6

Cable Rd.

Brackett Rd.

Tunnel

To Lecount Hollow Rd.

(5-mile extension)

HOW to get there

Take Route 6 from the north or south into Eastham. Watch for the sign SALT POND VISITOR CENTER.

No. 16 Eastham–Coast Guard Beach

you'd like to take a short side trip to Cape Cod Bay, continue straight ahead to First Encounter Beach. Return to Great Pond Road and proceed past the Town Landing and public beach on the shore of Great Pond.

Go uphill from Great Pond, continuing on Great Pond Road through a residential part of Eastham, back to Route 6, which will be about 1 mile from your turn onto this road from Samoset Road. When you arrive at Route 6, turn left and ride along the "bi-walk," an extra-wide sidewalk shared by pedestrians and bicyclists. In 0.75 mile, at the traffic light at Brackett Road, you'll see a large green sign that says NAUSET LIGHT BEACH—your next destination. Proceed across Route 6 and uphill on Brackett Road. In 1 mile at the T intersection with Nauset Road, turn left and then immediately right onto Cable Road to a bluff overlooking the ocean and Nauset Light Beach. In the event that the Nauset and Cable Road signs are missing, watch for the signs to Nauset Light Beach. The beach is below the bluff. As you leave the beach parking lot, turn left at the first intersection, Ocean View Drive. When Coast Guard Beach comes into sight, there is a sudden downhill at the bottom of which you must yield, so watch the traffic, then cross over the wooden bridge to the parking lot behind the former Coast Guard Station. From the observation areas to the side and front of the large white building, the view of the ocean and the tidal wetlands is spectacular. If you can get back here at sunset, do; the display of glorious colors is stunning.

After you have seen and experienced all you have time for, take the Nauset Trail bike path that begins just behind the former four-boat garage, which now houses changing and rest rooms. The bike path crosses two spur roads, and just before the first one you'll see the Doane Rock and picnic site. The bike path also crosses the Nauset Salt Marsh on a long, straight wooden bridge, a fine vantage point for a close-up look at an actual salt marsh. After 2 miles, mostly downhill, you arrive back at the Salt Pond Visitor Center.

GUGLIELMO MARCONI

THE PIONEER OF WIRELESS
COMMUNICATION
SON OF ITALY
CITIZEN OF THE WORLD

BORN IN BOLOGNA APRIL 25, 1874
DIED IN ROME   JULY 20, 1937

THE HON. EGIDIO ORTONA
AMBASSADOR OF ITALY TO THE U.S.A.
THE HON. JOHN A. VOLPE
AMBASSADOR OF THE U.S.A. TO ITALY
HONORARY CHAIRMAN
FRANCO FAÀ DI BRUNO
CONSUL GENERAL OF ITALY IN BOSTON
CHAIRMAN

South Wellfleet–
Marconi Station

Number of miles:	9.6
Approximate pedaling time:	1½ hours
Terrain:	Moderately hilly
Surface:	Very good
Things to see:	The Marconi Wireless Station, Marconi Beach, Wellfleet Bay Wildlife Sanctuary, Cape Cod National Seashore Headquarters

Leave your vehicle in the parking lot of the Cape Cod National Seashore Headquarters and ride out toward the ocean and the Marconi Station site. The approach is flat, almost like a plain. Then the road goes gently uphill to the top of a bluff. It is very quiet. Here, on this bluff, Guglielmo Marconi built his wireless station and sent the first wireless telegraph message across the Atlantic to England in 1903, a message from President Theodore Roosevelt to King Edward VII. There is a display that tells the fascinating story. As of September 1996 the large sculpture of the head of Marconi in the photograph on the left-hand page had been stolen twice and twice recovered. The National Seashore authorities are working on a security system that will safeguard this extraordinary work of art. Hopefully, it will be back on its pedestal when you read this.

When you can break away from the hypnotic pull of the horizon, lock up your bike and take the 1.25-mile nature trail to White Cedar Swamp and Forest, crossing the swamp on a boardwalk. The change from ocean and far horizon to swamp is swift, and the contrast is startling.

Retrace your route back, past the National Seashore Headquarters to the Y; turn left and head toward Marconi Beach. This great beach

No. 17 South Wellfleet–Marconi Station

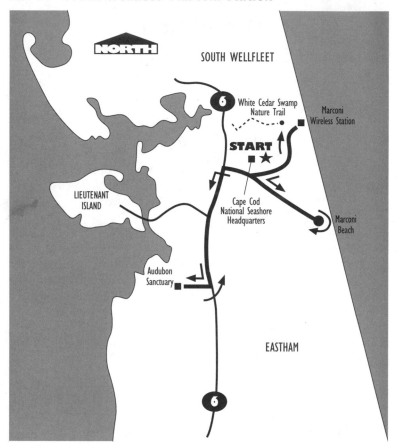

SOUTH WELLFLEET

NORTH

White Cedar Swamp Nature Trail

Marconi Wireless Station

START

LIEUTENANT ISLAND

Cape Cod National Seashore Headquarters

Marconi Beach

Audubon Sanctuary

EASTHAM

HOW to get there Proceed north on Route 6 to South Wellfleet. About 1.75 miles from the Eastham town line, turn right after the sign MARCONI AREA NEXT RIGHT. Proceed 0.5 mile to the Cape Cod National Seashore Headquarters.

is another of the lovingly preserved, fine white sand beaches of *your* Cape Cod National Seashore, stretching as far as the eye can see. The bathhouse facilities are designed low and of weathered gray board to complement, not intrude upon, the landscape, and there is a boardwalk with steps leading down to the beach.

When you are ready to continue, return, pass the headquarters again, and proceed to Route 6. Turn left onto Route 6 and proceed for 1.5 miles until you see the white-and-green sign featuring a herring gull and stating MASS. AUDUBON SOCIETY. Turn right and go straight ahead into the society's Wellfleet Bay Wildlife Sanctuary. It's open from 8:00 A.M. to 8:00 P.M., and there is a small fee.

There are picnic tables, rest rooms, and a bike road. Try to plan your day so that you have ample time to explore the nature trail on foot. In the office, the house to your left, you can pick up a map of the sanctuary. The area that is particularly exciting for nature lovers is Try Island, out in the marsh. Here you can see a landscape that is characteristic of the Cape and of the New England shore—great tidal wetlands. The island permits you to go out far into the marsh and experience the space, color, smell, and rhythm of the wetlands. If you buy guides for the sanctuary's specific walks, you will be greatly assisted in identifying the rich birdlife and flora of the marsh and woodlands. This is one of the few sites on the Cape that provide access to the wetlands.

When you leave the sanctuary, turn left at the gate and within a few yards you'll rejoin Route 6. Proceed for 1 mile back to the National Seashore Headquarters. Before you leave, go inside the building. It has exhibits, a supply of informative pamphlets, some very friendly and helpful U.S. National Park Service people—and rest rooms! The hours are 8:00 A.M. to 4:30 P.M. Monday through Friday.

South Wellfleet–
Lecount Hollow

Number of miles:	9.7
Approximate pedaling time:	1 hour
Terrain:	Definitely hilly
Surface:	Good
Things to see:	Typical Cape pine forest, Lecount Hollow Beach, Ocean View Beach, White Crest Beach, bluffs

This is a ride for beachcombing, beach walking, sitting and gazing, sand castle building, sunbathing, and/or swimming at one, two, or all three—Lecount Hollow Beach, Ocean View Beach, and White Crest Beach. All have rest rooms, open in summer only. The three beaches are part of the Cape Cod National Seashore, the 27,000-acre seashore that encompasses and protects an unbroken stretch of 30 miles of superb ocean beaches.

You can begin by parking in the Schooner's Cove restaurant parking lot, on the southeast corner of Route 6 and Gross Hill Road, and then heading south down Route 6 about 0.5 mile. Just past the cemetery on your left, turn left on Cahoon Hollow Road. Go uphill. It's short but very steep. Take the second road on the right, which is Old County Road. You will meander through a semiresidential area of dunes and a typical Cape pine forest. Old County Road is roughly parallel to Route 6. After about 1.5 miles a road comes in from the right. Continue straight ahead and rejoin Route 6. Turn left on Route 6, ride about 0.25 mile, and turn left onto Lecount Hollow Road. Ride straight to the ocean on this road. Lecount Hollow Beach will be at your feet. This is a lovely white beach bordered by the Cape's very special green-and-blue ocean. You can swim here, or you may prefer

No. 18 South Wellfleet–Lecount Hollow

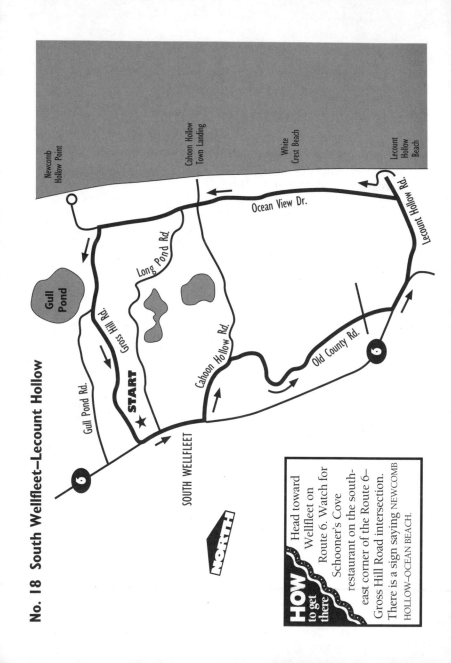

NORTH

HOW to get there Head toward Wellfleet on Route 6. Watch for Schooner's Cove restaurant on the south-east corner of the Route 6–Gross Hill Road intersection. There is a sign saying NEWCOMB HOLLOW–OCEAN BEACH.

Newcomb Hollow Point

Cahoon Hollow Town Landing

White Crest Beach

Lecount Hollow Beach

Ocean View Dr.

Gull Pond

Long Pond Rd.

Gross Hill Rd.

Gull Pond Rd.

START

Cahoon Hollow Rd.

Old County Rd.

Lecount Hollow Rd.

SOUTH WELLFLEET

6

6

to swim a little farther north of here, off Ocean View Drive, where there's a bit more privacy.

Head back down Lecount Hollow Road for a brief stretch to Ocean View Drive. Turn right. The crest yields a sensational view of beach, ocean, and bluffs dotted with summer cottages (some for rent; most private). There is a parking lot here, so ride in, lock your bike, and walk down to White Crest Beach. You can wander on foot all over the bluffs; you'll see numerous trails heading off through the scrub. Continue on Ocean View Drive after your swim.

When Cahoon Hollow Road crosses Ocean View, you could detour briefly by taking a right down the steep hill to the Town Landing. If you prefer not to, continue straight for a nice long downhill ride giving you stunning views off to your right.

Turn left on Gross Hill Road, which is very hilly, including a long uphill grade after the fork with Gull Pond Road. (Depending on the time of year, the Gross Hill Road sign may be missing, taken as a souvenir, so if you pass the turnoff onto Gross Hill, you will quickly come to a dead end at Newcomb Hollow Point. Go back and take the first road to the right, which is Gross Hill Road.) After about 2 miles on Gross Hill Road, you'll return to the intersection where you left your vehicle.

Wellfleet–Great Island

Number of miles:	6.8
Approximate pedaling time:	¾ hour
Terrain:	Hilly
Surface:	Good
Things to see:	Wellfleet, First Congregational Church, Wellfleet Historical Society Museum, the art galleries, Uncle Tim's Bridge, Wellfleet Harbor, Chequessett Neck, Great Island

History has it that the first European exploration of Cape Cod dates back as far as 1602, when Bartholomew Gosnold arrived from Falmouth, England, to chart and explore the American coast for the British Crown. He named the Cape for the cod his crew caught, and he left another mark for posterity by naming a large island with wild grapes growing on it Martha's Vineyard, after his daughter Martha.

What is now Wellfleet Harbor was visited in 1606 by the next explorer to sail across from Europe, Samuel de Champlain from France, who was so impressed by the oysters he found there that he named the harbor the "port with oysters." If you're adventurous, you too can shellfish for oysters on the harbor tidal flats at the twice-daily low tides. A shellfishing license is required; you can obtain one at the Town Hall, where you will start the ride.

So, after you have parked your vehicle or have arrived by bicycle, leave vehicle and/or bike locked up in the Town Hall parking lot and take a stroll down Main Street. Wellfleet is not very large—less than 2 miles wide—but it is considered one of the more tastefully developed resort towns on the Cape. One of the first things you will see is the First Congregational Church, a handsome building constructed in

No. 19 Wellfleet—Great Island

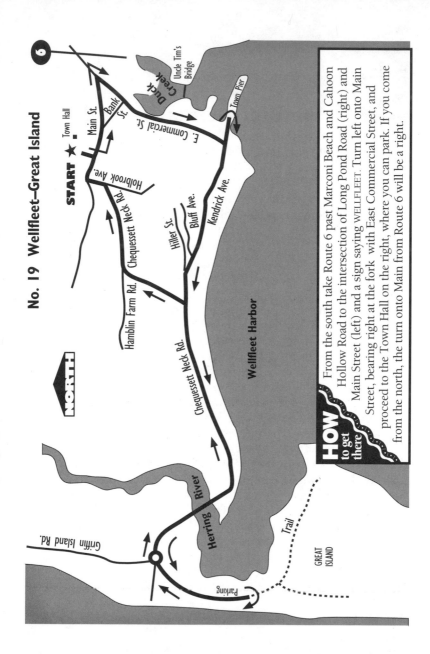

NORTH

START ★ Town Hall

Main St.

Bank St.

Duck Creek

Uncle Tim's Bridge

E. Commercial St.

Town Pier

Holbrook Ave.

Chequessett Neck Rd.

Hiller St.

Bluff Ave.

Kendrick Ave.

Hamblin Farm Rd.

Chequessett Neck Rd.

Wellfleet Harbor

Herring River

Griffin Island Rd.

Parking

Trail

GREAT ISLAND

HOW to get there

From the south take Route 6 past Marconi Beach and Cahoon Hollow Road to the intersection of Long Pond Road (right) and Main Street (left) and a sign saying WELLFLEET. Turn left onto Main Street, bearing right at the fork with East Commercial Street, and proceed to the Town Hall on the right, where you can park. If you come from the north, the turn onto Main from Route 6 will be a right.

1850 in the Greek Revival style, with an interior that is truly lovely. Take a look. If you happen to be there at one o'clock, you'll hear the clock in the steeple strike two—because it is the only town clock in the world that strikes on ship's time, per *Ripley's Believe It or Not*. One, five, and nine o'clock are "two bells." Farther down Main Street is the Wellfleet Historical Society Museum, a fine place in which to absorb the uniqueness of the town before you ride through it. The more than twenty art galleries you may see on your stroll will give credence to Wellfleet's claim to have become the art center of Cape Cod.

When you're ready, walk back for your bike, come out onto Main Street and turn left, riding 0.25 mile to a hairpin turn to the right onto East Commercial Street, which takes you down to Wellfleet Harbor, a large, beautifully protected anchorage that you can see in the distance. Before you get there, however, watch the left side of East Commercial Street for the sign and short road leading to "Uncle Tim's Bridge," the long, much-photographed footbridge over Duck Creek. It's just before Bank Street. Then continue on to the harbor. Ride out to the end of the pier at Shirttail Point to get the full effect of the village, the harbor (watched over by a white, spired church on a hill), and the dunes of Great Island, a preserve of the Cape Cod National Seashore.

Upon leaving the pier, take Kendrick Avenue west along the shore. As in every town on the Cape, here you'll pass an abundance of guest houses and motels. Bear left at the junction with Hiller Street and cross the Herring River. At the top of the hill, turn left into the Cape Cod National Seashore picnic grove and parking area. Here you will find written guides to the hiking trail on Great Island, also two portable toilets. This trail is an 8-mile round-trip, which you may want to do, provided you have hiking boots and good health. In any event walk some distance onto Great Island just to enjoy the ambience of this unique natural site.

To return to town, retrace your route along Chequessett Neck Road. Bear left at the Y, staying on Chequessett Neck Road. Chequessett Neck bears sharply right where Hamblin Farm Road comes in from your left. Stay on Chequessett Neck Road. At the T intersection with Holbrook Road, turn left and return to Main Street, where you turn right and go the short distance to the Town Hall.

Wellfleet–Truro

Number of miles:	14
Approximate pedaling time:	2 hours
Terrain:	Rolling up and down, curving left and right
Surface:	Old asphalt, generally good condition
Things to see:	Undeveloped and unspoiled Cape Cod, Cobb Memorial Library, Wellfleet art galleries, 1850 First Congregational Church

Many moons ago, stagecoaches were the only transportation from Wellfleet to Provincetown, and the quiet, narrow country road you will be riding on—a road that rarely goes in a straight line—is the road they used, the Old Truro Road.

To reach it, follow the "How to get there" directions to Main Street in Wellfleet and proceed past East Commercial and Bank streets on the left to the Town Hall, which will be on your right. If you have come by car, van, or some other type of bike carrier, park in the Town Hall's parking lot.

Now for a suggestion: Leave bike and vehicle locked up and take a leisurely stroll down Main Street. Wellfleet is a small town, with many interesting places to see—more than twenty art galleries, the Wellfleet Historical Society Museum, and the handsome First Congregational Church, built in 1850 in the Greek Revival style. Take a look inside: The interior is lovely. If you are there at one, five, or nine o'clock, the clock in the steeple will strike two—"two bells," because it is the only town clock in the world that strikes on ship's time! (For more information about the area, see Ride 19.)

No. 20 Wellfleet–Truro

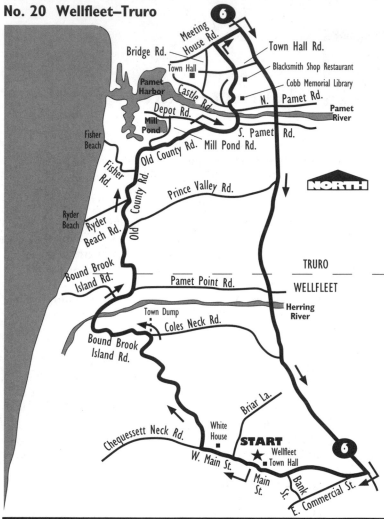

HOW to get there From the south take Route 6 past Marconi Beach and Cahoon Hollow Road to the intersection of Long Pond Road (right) and Main Street (left) and a sign saying WELLFLEET. Turn left onto Main Street, bearing right at the fork with East Commercial Street, and proceed to the Town Hall on the right, where you can park. If you come from the north, the turn onto Main from Route 6 will be a right.

This leisurely stroll through town may give you a nice feel for the contrast between Wellfleet, which was explored in 1602 by Bartholomew Goswold from Falmouth, England, and in 1606 by Samuel de Champlain from France, and the quiet, unspoiled, seemingly forgotten countryside between here and Truro.

Back at the Town Hall, check out your bicycle and, when ready, come out of the parking lot and turn right onto Main Street, which soon narrows and becomes West Main Street—which may not be so marked. After you pass Briar Lane on the right, the road makes a sharp right turn around a white frame house. This is Old Truro Road.

Soon you will pass the town Department of Public Works, and as you do you will enter a quiet world of the marsh, the fen, with hawks and ducks and seagulls calling and untouched bushes growing as they please. Ride slowly, for now you are on a roller coaster. A hard right turn, downhill, then left, passing the Yellow Brick Road on the right. In 1 mile you pass Coles Neck Road coming in from your right. You go hard left, now on Bound Brook Road, then right, then left and right again, another left, and a ninety-degree right, passing Bound Brook Island Road on the left. Right about here you should see a sign indicating Wellfleet to the rear and Truro straight ahead. You are now 3.2 miles from your turn at the white frame house and on Old County Road.

You curve left as Pamet Point Road comes in from the right. You are still on Old County Road; it carries you into Truro, which you can tell by the end of the marshes, as the still narrow road rises into Truro's moors with wild cranberry and now old Cape homes nestled among the hillocks.

Prince Valley Road curves in from the right, followed by Ryder Beach Road on the left. You are just about 4 miles from the turn at that famous white house. If you want to take a break on the beach, turn left on Ryder Beach Road. There's no fee for bikes, and there are rest rooms.

Next you'll come to Fisher Road. It goes off to the left to Fisher Beach—which doesn't have rest rooms.

Continue up on Old County Road around to the right, past Mill Pond Road, skirting Mill Pond itself, past Depot Road, which came in at a forty-five-degree angle from the left. Castle Road is the next road on the left, across from the Cobb Memorial Library. This is a good place to do a "stop and look." Before you go in the library, take a look at the tree just past it. It made me think of a giant glockenspiel without the flat metal bars in the center.

Continue the ride, shifting your gears for the steep hill, passing by the Blacksmith Shop Restaurant on the right. At the rise of the hill, there's an intersection with a road going off to the right over a bridge to Route 6. You continue around to the left, past Town Hall Road, curving downhill to a T intersection with Bridge Road, which joins with Meeting House Road and brings you out to Route 6.

This is the halfway point of the ride, where you have a choice of either riding back to Wellfleet on the 6-foot-wide shoulder of Route 6 or returning the way you came, which can give you a different perspective of the countryside as you ride back to Wellfleet. The advantage of the Route 6 return is that it is 1.25 miles shorter.

North Truro—
The Highlands

Number of miles:	9.8
Approximate pedaling time:	1½ hours
Terrain:	Hilly
Surface:	Good
Things to see:	Head of Meadow Beach, Highland Light, Highland House Museum, Jenny Lind Tower, both coasts of the Cape

The town of Truro, including North and South Truro, is one of the largest towns in terms of area and the smallest in population—about 1,500 year round. Many of those residents are artists and writers attracted, as was Edward Hopper, by the Cape light and landscape.

The ride begins at the end of High Head Road, which becomes a dirt road soon after it leaves Route 6, at the point where it forks. Here you go left, following the sign that reads PARKING. At the end of this road is a tiny parking lot with a sign at its far end that reads OVER SAND ROUTES—ANNUAL PERMIT REQUIRED. Hidden to the right is the entrance to the Head of the Meadow Bicycle Trail. Start the ride here and take off on your bike onto the fine, paved, bikes-only trail, which wanders through the scrub oak and pine forest along the edge of Salt Meadow. It runs for a marvelous 2 miles and comes out at Head of Meadow Beach. After a visit to the beach, ride down Head of Meadow Beach Road toward Route 6. When you reach Route 6, turn left and then go off Route 6 to the right, down a short hill, and then left onto Highland Road, which passes under Route 6. You'll see a sign here to HIGHLANDS—1 MILE.

Highlands means just that, so expect a long incline that levels off in 0.5 mile and then continues up a slight grade to a T intersection with a sign that reads HIGHLAND LIGHT. Turn right, go up a short hill, and

No. 21 North Truro–The Highlands

HOW to get there

From the south take Route 6 to High Head Road, at the eastern end of Pilgrim Lake. Depending on the season, the HIGH HEAD ROAD sign may be missing, so watch for the sign reading TO RTE. 6A BEACH POINTS, with a left-pointing arrow. Turn right just after that sign.

Pilgrim Lake

6A

6A

START

High Head Rd.

Head of Meadow Beach

Head of the Meadow Beach Rd.

Windigo La.

6

Cobb Rd.

Pond St.

Knowles Heights Rd.

Highland Rd.

Tunnel

S. Hollow Rd.

Highland Light

Jenny Lind Tower

USAF Radar Domes

6

NORTH

then turn left. You can see the Highland Lighthouse ahead of you. The Highland House Museum is on your left. Run by the Truro Historical Society- it contains everyday articles used by the Pilgrims (such as firearms and relics from shipwrecks). It is open from 1:30 to 4:30 P.M. daily in the summer; a small admission fee is charged. Continue up to the Highland Light (also called the Cape Cod Light). It now flashes a four-million-candlepower beacon, warning ships—today mostly huge, heavily laden oil tankers—away from the "Graveyard of Ships."

It was originally built in 1798 and was then destroyed by fire and rebuilt in 1857. For 98 years it sat in the same spot on the cliff, beaming its light 30 miles out to sea, but the relentless pounding of the storm waves have been steadily eroding the cliff and it would have fallen into the ocean if it stayed where it was. In 1961 it was 232 feet from the cliff. In mid 1990 it was but 128 feet from the edge.

So The Truro Historical Society formed the Committee to Save The Cape Cod Light, locally known as the Highland Light, in 1990 with the intention to move it 450 feet inland—a massive undertaking, considering that the lighthouse weighed approximately 400 tons. It was accomplished nevertheless and in the late summer of 1996 it was moved 450 feet inland. The lighthouse keeper's house was also moved and the wooden outlook platform is being rebuilt with a walkway to it from the Lighthouse. From the overlook you can see both sides of the Cape, ocean and bay. As you walk to the overlook, you'll see the Jenny Lind Tower—a quirky thing!—and beyond the tower, like enormous, frightfully expensive golf balls, the radar domes of an Air Force Radar Station. In 1850 Jenny Lind, the "Swedish Nightingale," came to Boston for a concert. More tickets were sold than there were seats. To prevent a riot, Jenny climbed to the top of this tower, so the story goes, and sang to the crowd. In 1927 one Harry Aldrich bought the tower and moved it here.

Retrace your tracks and go downhill to the intersection, where you turn left on South Highland Road and ride downhill. At the bottom of the grade, turn right on South Hollow Road. This is a pleasant road, with no houses on either side, that winds its quiet way through stunted pines for a mile, until it comes to Route 6. Go across Route 6 to the T intersection with Route 6A, just a few feet from 6, and turn right. This is a pretty stiff uphill for 0.25 mile, at which point the road crests and starts to roll up and down.

At approximately 1.2 miles from your turn onto 6A, you'll come to Windigo Lane on the left. Turn left onto it. (Disregard the PRIVATE WAY part of the Windigo Lane street sign.) You are on a bluff; wind around for a short stretch, to Cobb Road. Turn left onto Cobb and then right where it forms a T with Knowles Heights Road. Stay on Knowles Heights Road as it wanders for 1.5 miles through these dunes, along the Cape Cod Bay shore, until it rejoins 6A at the bottom of the short, steep downgrade. Where 6A intersects with Route 6, turn left and then right where you see the sign HIGH HEAD. Go up High Head Road to the parking lot where you left your vehicle.

Province Lands

Number of miles:	8.75
Approximate pedaling time:	1 hour
Terrain:	Hilly
Surface:	Excellent
Things to see:	Herring Cove Beach, sand dunes, ponds, bogs, Race Point Beach, Province Lands Visitors' Center

To reach the starting point of the bike path, ride through the one-row vehicle parking lot that is on the right side of the Herring Cove Beach bathhouse when you are facing the ocean, to the far end. (The rest rooms in the bathhouse are open in the early spring.)

The ride is on a specially laid-out asphalt bike path that takes you up and down spectacular sand dunes and pitch pine forests to the Atlantic Ocean side of the tip of the Cape and then loops back through dramatically contrasting terrain.

When we rode it, in September after Labor Day, we turned left at the first fork, just past the first underpass under Province Lands Road, and went clockwise around the circuit. The Cape Cod National Seashore staff recommends a counterclockwise circuit from this first fork, however. In summer, when more bikers are in blossom, it is probably wiser to follow their suggestion, although the path is wide enough to pass other bicyclists. There are some great downhills with sharp curves; keep to the right and stay alert.

The area you are passing through was set aside by the Plimouth Colony in 1620, a remarkable act on the part of these hardy folk, pre-occupied as they must have been with sheer survival. There are several places to stop and spend some pleasurable time picnicking and/or swimming at either of the two beaches, visiting the Province

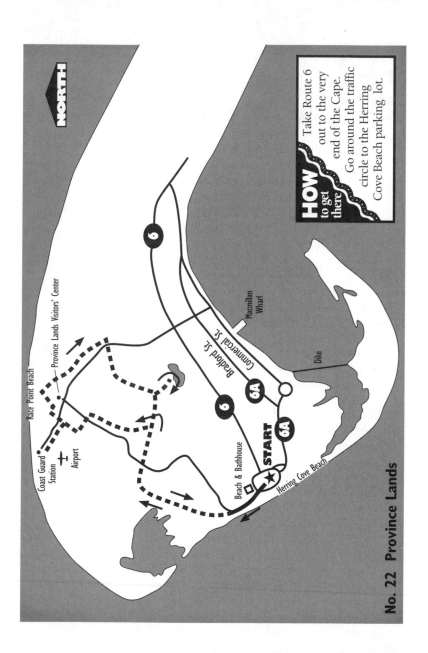

NORTH

Province Lands Visitors' Center

Race Point Beach

Coast Guard Station

Airport

Beach & Bathhouse

START

Herring Cove Beach

6

6

6A

6A

Bradford St.

Commercial St.

Macmillan Wharf

Dike

HOW to get there

Take Route 6 out to the very end of the Cape. Go around the traffic circle to the Herring Cove Beach parking lot.

No. 22 Province Lands

Lands Visitors' Center, taking the nature walk in the Beach Forest area—or taking a bargain-priced sightseeing flight from the Provincetown Municipal Airport in a classic 1930 "Stinson Detroiter" airliner!

The visitors' center is up a steep hill from either direction, and the panoramic view from the observation deck is worth the climb. There is an outdoor theater (closed after Labor Day), and inside, movies about the area and its wildlife are shown every hour on the hour.

The Beach Forest Trail is a 1-mile loop that is well worth taking. Be sure you can lock your bike securely before you set out afoot. The walk is beautifully described in detail in *Short Walks on Cape Cod and the Vineyard,* by Hugh and Heather Sadlier (Globe Pequot Press).

This is one of the nicest rides on the Cape, with short, roller-coaster hills, unique scenery, and *no* automobiles to contend with.

Provincetown

Number of miles:	8.5
Approximate pedaling time:	1½ hours
Terrain:	Slightly hilly
Surface:	Good
Things to see:	The myriad wonders of Provincetown! Macmillan Wharf, Provincetown Aquarium, Pilgrim Monument and Museum, Seth Nickerson House, Herring Cove Beach

This ride will take you on a tour of fabulous Provincetown with its old houses, historic landmarks, fishing fleet, and artists and artisans of all descriptions. After riding from Herring Cove Beach to the rotary, before you enter the town proper, lock up your bike and walk out on the dike built to protect Provincetown Harbor. The dike, which goes over to Long Point, yields a fine view of the harbor.

The street coming out of Provincetown to this point is one-way, so you can't use it; instead, continue around the rotary, retracing your route to the point where 6A heads into town. Turn right at 6A SOUTH–PROVINCETOWN CENTER–BOSTON. This is West Bradford Street. There are two principal streets in Provincetown: Bradford Street, which is two-way, and Commercial Street, which parallels the harbor and is one-way.

As you ride along Bradford, you'll pass numerous narrow lanes running between Bradford and Commercial. (You will be returning along the waterfront on Commercial Street.) Bradford is lined with guest houses of all shapes, sizes, and qualities and with little restaurants. You'll pass the David Fairbanks House (1776) and the Folk

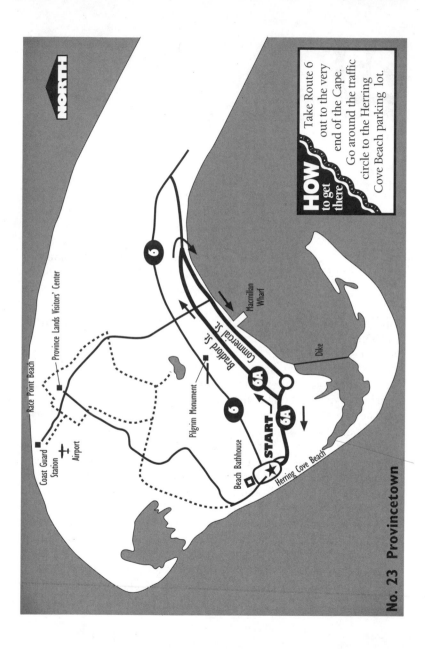

NORTH

HOW to get there
Take Route 6 out to the very end of the Cape. Go around the traffic circle to the Herring Cove Beach parking lot.

Race Point Beach

Province Lands Visitors' Center

Coast Guard Station

Airport

Pilgrim Monument

Beach Bathhouse

START

Herring Cove Beach

6A

6A

Bradford St.

Commercial St.

Macmillan Wharf

Dike

6

6

No. 23 Provincetown

Museum. At Winslow Street, 3 miles from the start of the ride, turn left and ride up to the Pilgrim Monument and Museum. If you're in good shape, climb up to the top. The view is worth it!

As you come to the end of Bradford, you'll pass craft shops, and there will be dozens more of these on Commercial Street. At the junction with Commercial, make a hairpin turn to the right and head back along the waterfront. At this end of town, many small cottages are jammed cheek-to-jowl along the road.

About a mile from the Bradford-Commercial intersection, you'll reach the downtown area. Restaurants, galleries, and shops are piled on each other. Leatherwork, silverwork, antique jewelry, paintings, prints, portraits done in a single sitting—all are available here. Throngs of pedestrians make riding in this narrow street almost impossible; you'll probably find you'd rather get off your bike and push it along through the center of town—or lock it up while you stroll here, joining the vacationers in a snack or drink at such places as the Inn at the Mews or the Café Blasé (located next to one of several bike rental shops).

Macmillan Wharf is at the 5-mile point on the ride. Go out on the wharf, where, if you can be here at 6:00 A.M., you can watch the commercial fishermen unloading their catches. If you have the time to spare, take a whale watch cruise on one of the boats that offer this unique experience. (*Note:* There are rest rooms at the land end of Macmillan Wharf.) Down past the wharf there are numerous additional craftspeople and portrait painters. Soon you'll pass Town Hall Square; the site of the Provincetown Playhouse, which now houses many, many small shops; and Union Square, with its many shops.

Turn left where Commercial Street goes almost ninety degrees to the left at the 6-mile point. You'll come to the town landing and Provincetown's oldest house, built circa 1746, at 72 Commercial Street. The house is open to the public. This end of Commercial Street has a number of quaint, older houses. A lovely inn, the Red Inn, is located here—it's open year-round and serves dinner nightly.

You'll come out at the rotary at the dike after 6.5 miles. Turn right and continue back toward your vehicle in the Herring Cove Beach parking lot.

Combination:
Osterville–Centerville & Hyannis

Number of miles:	27.5
Approximate pedaling time:	4 hours
Terrain:	Mostly flat; a few moderate hills
Surface:	Good
Things to see:	Towns of Osterville, Centerville, and Hyannis; Hyannis Harbor; 1856 Country Store; Centerville Historical Museum; Craigville Beach; Kalmus Park Beach

This ride combines Ride 6, Osterville–Centerville, with Ride 7, Hyannis. Since the rides overlap for the 0.25-mile section of Centerville's Main Street, if you start in Osterville (page 21), ride all the way around to Centerville's exceptional Main Street. After you have visited the 1856 Country Store and arrived at the traffic light at the intersection with South Main and Craigville Beach Road straight ahead, instead of turning right onto South Main, turn left. In less than a mile, Pine Street will merge in from the left and then merge with West Main Street; bear right and you are now on the Hyannis ride. Follow its directions until you arrive back at the intersection of Craigville Beach Road, Main Street, and South Main Street, whereupon you turn left and get back on the Osterville–Centerville ride, on your way back to the starting place.

If you begin from Hyannis (page 25), when you get to the intersection of Craigville Beach Road, Main Street, and South Main Street, turn left on South Main Street, toward Osterville. Do the Osterville–Centerville ride around to its colorful Main Street and then get back onto the Hyannis ride by turning left onto South Main Street.

Be sure to check the map for this combo ride when you come to the place where the rides join.

No. 24 Combination

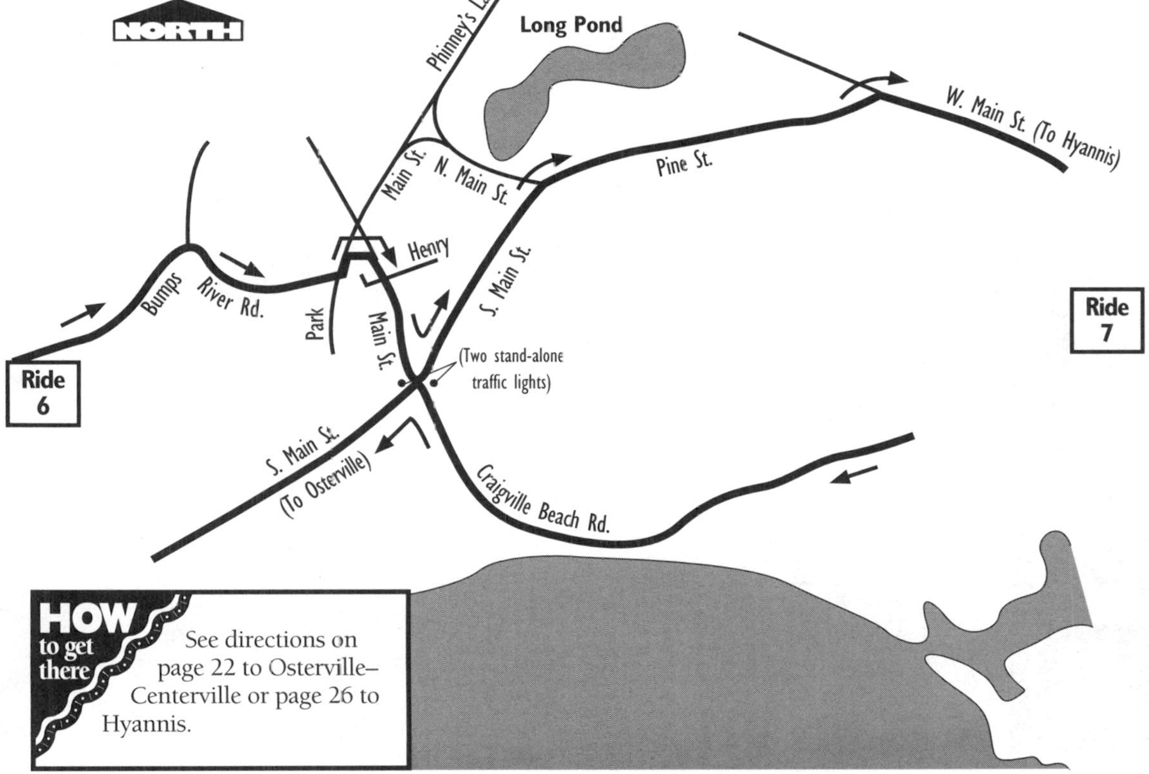

NORTH

Long Pond

Phinney's La.

Main St.

N. Main St.

Pine St.

S. Main St.

W. Main St. (To Hyannis)

Ride 7

Henry

Main St.

Park

(Two stand-alone traffic lights)

Craigville Beach Rd.

S. Main St. (To Osterville)

River Rd.

Bumps

Ride 6

HOW to get there

See directions on page 22 to Osterville–Centerville or page 26 to Hyannis.

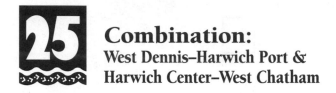

Combination:
West Dennis–Harwich Port &
Harwich Center–West Chatham

Number of miles:	32
Approximate pedaling time:	4 hours
Terrain:	Flat to hilly
Surface:	Good
Things to see:	The villages of Harwich Center, Harwich Port, and West Dennis; Cape Cod Rail Trail; Wychmere Harbor; several fine beaches

This ride combines Ride 9, West Dennis–Harwich Port, with Ride 10, Harwich Center–West Chatham. The rides overlap at the intersection of Route 124 and Main Street in Harwich Center. Therefore, if you begin with Ride 9 at its starting point at the intersection of Route 28 and Trotting Park Road, when you reach the intersection of Route 124 and Main Street in Harwich Center, you will be at the starting point of Ride 10. Follow the directions for Ride 10; go left on Main, then right onto Chatham Road, and so on, until you arrive once again at the intersection of Route 124 and Main Street. Now you follow the directions for the last half of Ride 9; go left on Main Street for the short distance to Bank Street, where you turn right, and so forth, until you come back to the starting point at the intersection of Route 28 and Trotting Park Road.

No. 25 Combination

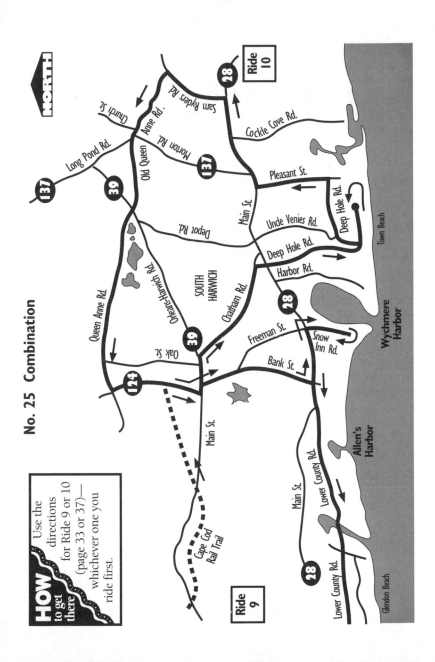

NORTH

HOW to get there: Use the directions for Ride 9 or 10 (page 33 or 37)—whichever one you ride first.

Ride 10

Ride 9

137

137

39

39

28

28

28

Church St.

Long Pond Rd.

Sam Ryders Rd.

Anne Rd.

Morton Rd.

Old Queen Anne Rd.

Cockle Cove Rd.

Pleasant St.

Main St.

Uncle Venies Rd.

Depot Rd.

Deep Hole Rd.

Deep Hole Rd.

Harbor Rd.

Queen Anne Rd.

Orleans-Harwich Rd.

SOUTH HARWICH

Chatham Rd.

Oak St.

Freeman St.

Snow Inn Rd.

Bank St.

Main St.

Cape Cod Rail Trail

Main St.

Lower County Rd.

Lower County Rd.

Wychmere Harbor

Town Beach

Allen's Harbor

Glendon Beach

Combination:
Province Lands & Provincetown

Number of miles:	17.25
Approximate pedaling time:	2½ to 6 hours
Terrain:	Half flat, half hilly
Surface:	Excellent
Things to see:	Spectacular sand dunes, ponds, bogs, Herring Cove and Race Point beaches, Province Lands Visitors' Center, the myriad wonders of Provincetown

This ride combines Ride 22, Province Lands, with Ride 23, Provincetown.

The two rides overlap at the starting place, which is the same for each: the Herring Cove Beach parking lot. You can begin with either one. My personal choice is to first experience the peace and tranquility of the dunes and then, with soul refreshed and fortified, plunge into the hurly-burly of fabulous Provincetown.

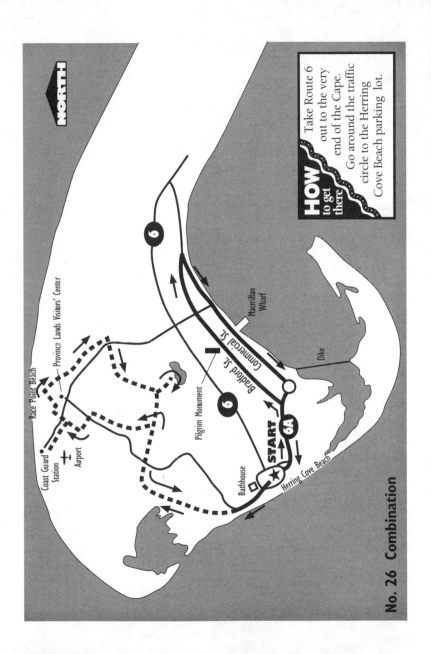

NORTH

HOW to get there
Take Route 6 out to the very end of the Cape. Go around the traffic circle to the Herring Cove Beach parking lot.

Province Lands Visitors' Center

Race Point Beach

Coast Guard Station

Airport

Pilgrim Monument

Bradford St.

Commercial St.

MacMillan Wharf

Dike

6

6

START

6A

Bathhouse

Herring Cove Beach

No. 26 Combination

Oak Bluffs/Vineyard Haven–Edgartown (Martha's Vineyard)

Number of miles:	20.5
Approximate pedaling time:	2½ hours
Terrain:	Flat to moderately hilly
Surface:	Good
Things to see:	Joseph Sylvia State Beach, Wesleyan Grove Campground, East Chop, the Flying Horses Carousel, Felix Neck Wildlife Sanctuary, Ocean Park

Martha's Vineyard is an island with two personas: In the high season it scintillates as the population burgeons from 7,000 to 70,000; in the off-season it becomes a different place, quieter, more tranquil, and serene.

This ride will give you the opportunity to experience two of the three major towns, Vineyard Haven and Oak Bluffs. They are delightfully different from each other. You can begin in either Vineyard Haven or Oak Bluffs, depending on the season and the ferry you take. Car and passenger ferries will take you to Vineyard Haven year-round and to Oak Bluffs from late May through September 15 from Woods Hole. During the same period, May to September, passenger (and bicycle) ferries from Hyannis and Falmouth on the Cape and from New Bedford serve Vineyard Haven and Oak Bluffs.

If you land at Oak Bluffs, begin the ride where you get off the ferry, at the junction of Bluffs Avenue and Seaview Avenue. Go to the right, riding up to the end of the point on Seaview. Circle the point to take in all the maneuvers as boats motor in and out of Oak Bluffs Harbor. If you're lucky, you might see a sailboat coming in or going out without using its engine—under full sail. It's tricky and a great way to show off if you know how to do it. I got lucky and did it in two different harbors because I had to: My engine had died!

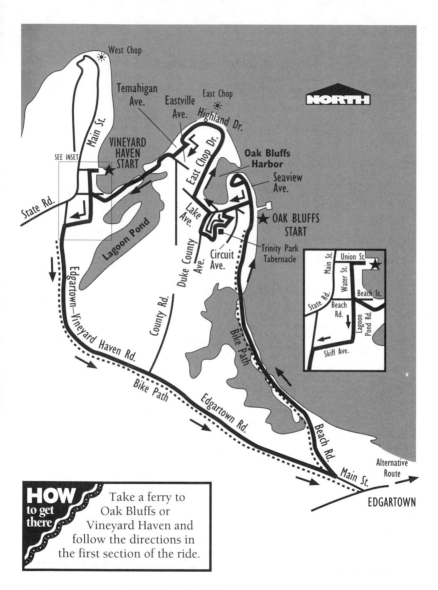

West Chop

Temahigan Ave.

Eastville Ave.

East Chop

Highland Dr.

Main St.

VINEYARD HAVEN START

SEE INSET

East Chop Dr.

Oak Bluffs Harbor

Seaview Ave.

State Rd.

Lagoon Pond

Lake Ave.

OAK BLUFFS START

Duke County Ave.

Circuit Ave.

Trinity Park Tabernacle

NORTH

Union St.

Main St.

Water St.

Beach St.

State Rd.

Beach Rd.

Lagoon Pond Rd.

Skiff Ave.

Edgartown–Vineyard Haven Rd.

County Rd.

Bike Path

Bike Path

Edgartown Rd.

Beach Rd.

Main St.

Alternative Route

EDGARTOWN

HOW to get there

Take a ferry to
Oak Bluffs or
Vineyard Haven and
follow the directions in
the first section of the ride.

No. 27 Oak Bluffs–Vineyard Haven

When you've seen enough, come back up Seaview, turn right onto Bluffs Avenue, and follow Bluffs to Circuit. Stop here for a walking tour of Circuit Avenue on the left. Circuit is Oak Bluff's main street; bikes are not allowed. At the intersection you'll see a carousel called "Flying Horses." Don't miss it (open Friday, Saturday, and Sunday only)!

Mount up again, head down Bluffs Avenue, and turn left onto Central Avenue. This little street will take you uphill to the Martha's Vineyard Campmeeting Association. At the top of the hill, bear left, then right on Montgomery Avenue to come out at Trinity Park Tabernacle. Turn right and circle around the tabernacle. Explore this unique community of narrow streets crowded with ornate, colorful, tiny cottages. After making the circuit, turn right onto Highland Avenue at the foot of Tabernacle Park and then right again onto Siloam Avenue. Siloam joins Duke County Avenue. Bear right and proceed to Lake Avenue. Sunset Lake is on the left.

Turn left onto Lake Avenue, which borders Oak Bluffs Harbor, and then right onto East Chop Drive, which goes alongside the water and then up a short hill. Go up onto the bluff and around the point of land called East Chop on Highland Drive and Atlantic Avenue. You'll pass the East Chop Lighthouse and then enjoy a downhill that yields a fabulous view. Your road goes sharply left soon after this, and then you turn right on Temahigan Avenue, which comes in from the left.

When Temahigan makes a T with Eastville Avenue, turn right. Eastville may not be marked. If it isn't, use the Martha's Vineyard Hospital, which is across the road in front of you, as a marker. Next, turn almost immediately left onto Beach Road, which takes you alongside the harbor over the causeway to Vineyard Haven. Beach Road follows the contour of the harbor, right then left, past Water Street on the right, to the fork with Main and Edgartown Road. (Note: If you landed at Vineyard Haven, you join the ride at this point. To get here, turn left onto Water Street as soon as you debark from the ferry, and ride straight to the Five Corners intersection, the wildest one I've ever encountered! No traffic lights, no stop signs, no police—it's every man, woman, and child for themselves. Go straight across—very carefully—to Lagoon Pond Road, which will take you to Skiff

Avenue by jogging a bit to the right and then to the left to Skiff, which goes straight to Edgartown Road.

Turn left onto Edgartown Road and ride across to the bike path on the right side of the road. It's a two-way street for bicycles, so keep to the right side of the path, which will give you 6.5 miles of car-, truck-, and moped-free road to Edgartown.

If you like nature walks, there is the Felix Neck Wildlife Sanctuary, about 1.5 miles from the County Road intersection on the left. Two miles farther you'll come to the outskirts of Edgartown, where Beach Road joins Edgartown Road from the left. There's a sign reading BIKE RTE. CROSSING. Continue on into Edgartown if you want to explore the town, which you can do by following the very specific directional signs for bicycles, such as ALL BICYCLES MUST TURN RIGHT (or LEFT) and BICYCLES: DO NOT ENTER. Edgartown has but four main streets—8 blocks long—and ten cross-streets. It's small, but it reflects the elegance of the prosperous nineteenth century, with many Federal-style homes.

When you are ready to continue on to Oak Bluffs or Vineyard Haven, ride out Main Street to the Y with Beach Road; turn right and north to another paved bike path that parallels Beach Road and the water for the 5-mile trip to Oak Bluffs. You'll soon see Sengekontacket Pond on your left and the beach for Edgartown residents on the right. The beach on the other side of the bridge over the inlet to Sengekontacket Pond is Sylvia State Beach, where you can swim, fish, and/or picnic. Continue north toward Oak Bluffs. The bike path ends at Seaview Avenue, so ride along Seaview to the Oak Bluffs ferry landing.

To get back to Vineyard Haven, follow the directions to Eastville Road and then retrace your route to Vineyard Haven.

Chappaquiddick (Martha's Vineyard)

Number of miles:	7.5
Approximate pedaling time:	1 hour
Terrain:	Flat to rolling
Surface:	Fair
Things to see:	East Beach, Cape Poge Light, Wasque Wildlife Preservation Area, On Time Ferry, Mytoi, Dyke Bridge

To reach Chappaquiddick Island, you must first come over to Martha's Vineyard, landing at either Vineyard Haven or Oaks Bluff. Both towns have nice long bike paths, 6 and 5 miles long, respectively, that take you directly to Edgartown and thence to Chappaquiddick.

If you land at Vineyard Haven, turn left onto Water Street as soon as you debark, and ride the short distance to the Five Corners intersection, where, with extreme caution, you go straight across onto Lagoon Pond Road, which takes you to Skiff Avenue, where you turn right and go for about 4 blocks until you come to Edgartown Road. Here you pick up the 6-mile bike path to Edgartown. If you land at Oak Bluffs, simply turn left onto Beach Road, which will also give you a bike path to Edgartown. This one runs along the seashore, is 5 miles long, and converges with the other path at Main Street in Edgartown.

Ride down Main Street, following the signs reading BIKE ROUTE TO CHAPPY FERRY. Don't despair—you're getting there!

Now you are ready to take a very short boat ride on a very small ferry, the On Time Ferry, so named because, lacking a fixed schedule, it is always on time. It will accommodate up to four automobiles plus lots of bikes and goes back and forth continually from 7:30 A.M. until midnight May 31 to October 15 and until 6:00 P.M. the rest of the year. The round-trip fares, as of August 1, 1996, are $3.00 for bike

No. 28 Chappaquiddick

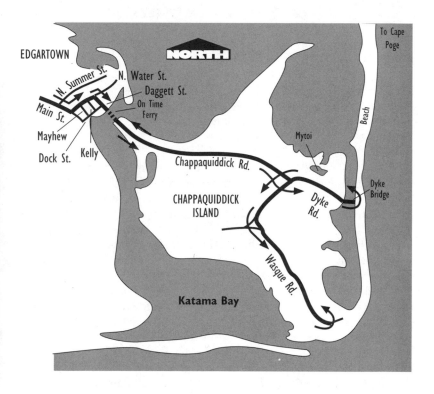

HOW to get there Take a ferry to Oak Bluffs or Vineyard Haven and follow directions in Ride 27, Oak Bluffs/ Vineyard Haven, to Main Street at the edge of Edgartown. Then follow the signs to the Chappaquiddick Ferry.

and rider and $5.00 for car and driver, plus $1.00 per passenger. The passage takes only a minute, so savor every second of the view of Edgartown, with its elegant captains' houses and lighthouse, and of Edgartown Harbor, dotted with boats of all kinds. To your right is Katama Bay.

Debark onto Chappaquiddick and proceed straight ahead; in the summer there will be many bicycles, and they are instructed to KEEP RIGHT. RIDE SINGLE FILE. You'll go by a beach club on the left and Caleb's Inlet on the right. The route goes up an incline. Be sure to pause at the top for the view of Edgartown and its environs. At about the 2-mile point, Chappaquiddick Road curves sharply right ninety degrees. Straight ahead is an unpaved dirt/sand road. This is Dyke Road. Take it and it will lead you to the site of the Dyke Bridge, which became a part of our history as the scene of an accident in 1969 in which a young woman drowned in a car driven by Edward Kennedy. The small bridge was dismantled in 1991 and rebuilt in 1995–1996. The new bridge is massively built. The original had no guardrails; the replacement has, and they appear to be made of 12-inch-square hardwood so solidly fastened together that no car or truck could ever break through. I doubt that even an army tank could do so. Now it is once again possible to cross over the inlet to Cape Poge and East Beach, a beautiful white sand beach on the Atlantic.

There is something else to see and spend time at along Dyke Road. It's on the left side, about halfway down, and if you haven't already visited it on your way down, be sure to stop on your return and spend time at Mytoi, an exquisite Japanese garden built on a fourteen-acre plot of land by one Mary Wakeman in the 1950s and willed to the Trustees of Reservations, which preserves and maintains the three-acre park. Ms. Wakeman called it "Mytoi" because it was her favorite toy. The newspaper *Vineyard Summer* calls it "a delightfully eccentric little pocket of the Orient on Chappaquiddick." Although Hurricane Bob devastated Mytoi in 1991, wiping out 60 percent of the trees and 50 percent of the flowers and shrubs, a five-year replanting program was begun right away and the garden is once again a tranquil place to renew one's spirit. The trustees also keep up the walking trail on the eleven acres of land across the road from Mytoi.

When you come to paved Chappaquiddick Road again, turn left. Here the road is also called School Road. Take it to a T intersection with Wasque Road on the left (paved) and Litchfield Road on the right (unpaved). Turn left onto Wasque Road. It soon becomes a dirt/sand road, so you have to ride carefully. Like many other roads on Martha's Vineyard, Wasque Road has many private roads leading from it. Continue to Wasque Point, where the 150-acre Wasque Reservation is open to the public. When you come to a fork and one-way signs, take the road that goes right ninety degrees to the beach. Return to the School Road junction after exploring Wasque Point, turn right, and ride back to the On Time Ferry. When you are back on the shore of Edgartown, if you have the time and inclination to explore this small town, bear in mind that the town fathers and mothers have established definite routes for bikes with the use of signs such as ALL BIKES MUST TURN RIGHT (OR LEFT) and BIKES DO NOT ENTER, etc. Turn right onto North Water Street from Daggett by walking your bike up to Water, and ride up past that fine old Victorian hotel and the Edgartown Lighthouse to Starbuck Neck Road where you hang a left up to Fuller and another left onto Fuller, then a brief right on Morse followed by a left onto North Summer. There are only four principal streets—Water, Summer, School, and Pease Way—so enjoy. When you're ready to go back to wherever you came from, wend your way back up Main Street to the place where the two bike paths come together. I suggest that you take the right path along the sea to Oaks Bluff even if you came down on the other one from Vineyard Haven, because although they're about the same distance to Vineyard Haven, the bike path up Edgartown–Vineyard Haven Road is uphill all the way! Just follow the directions and map of Ride 27, Oak Bluffs/Vineyard Haven.

Godspeed and may the wind be at your back!

Edgartown–Katama (South) Beach (Martha's Vineyard)

Number of miles:	10.5
Approximate pedaling time:	1¼ hours
Terrain:	Flat to moderately hilly
Surface:	Fair
Things to see:	Numerous captains' houses, Thomas Cooke House Museum, First Federated Church, Edgartown Lighthouse, On Time Ferry, Sheriff's Meadow, Katama (South) Beach

In 1671 Thomas Mayhew, who owned all of Martha's Vineyard and had founded the town in 1642, decided to name it after Edgar, the three-year-old son of the duke of York who was next in line to become the king.

Edgartown was a whaling town, and the whaling ship captains made huge fortunes from the oil of the whales they killed during those incredibly long voyages of two years or more, using their earnings to build elegant houses for themselves in the eighteenth and nineteenth centuries. Their houses still exist along Edgartown's narrow streets, many with widow's walks where the captains' wives kept vigil, eyes turned toward the sea, searching the horizon for the sight of a sail. Today Edgartown is a well-kept town whose chic boutiques and shops attract a youthful, upscale crowd, many of whom arrive on private yachts to stroll, shop, and see the sights. If you arrived on a bicycle, however, I will assume that you have come to the island by ferry, landing either at Vineyard Haven or at Oaks Bluff. If it's Vineyard Haven, to get to Edgartown turn left onto Water Street as soon as you debark, and ride the short distance to the wild and wooly Five Corners intersection, where, since there are neither traffic lights nor stop

No. 29 Edgartown–Katama

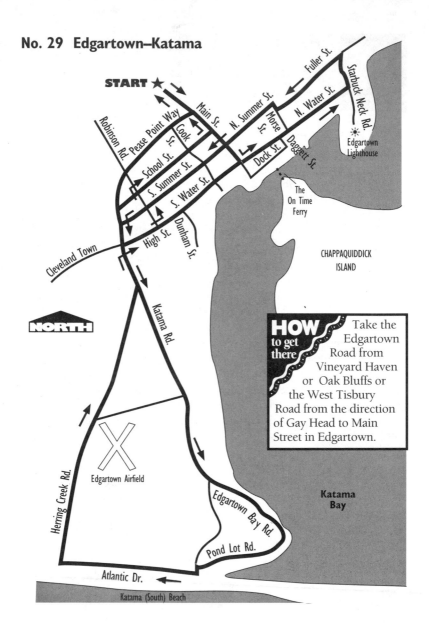

START ★

Fuller St.

Starbuck Neck Rd.

Main St.

N. Summer St.

N. Water St.

Robinson Rd.

Pease Point Way

Cook St.

Morse St.

Edgartown Lighthouse

School St.

Dock St.

Daggett St.

S. Summer St.

S. Water St.

The On Time Ferry

Dunham St.

CHAPPAQUIDDICK ISLAND

Cleveland Town

High St.

NORTH

Katama Rd.

Herring Creek Rd.

Edgartown Airfield

Edgartown Bay Rd.

Pond Lot Rd.

Katama Bay

HOW to get there Take the Edgartown Road from Vineyard Haven or Oak Bluffs or the West Tisbury Road from the direction of Gay Head to Main Street in Edgartown.

Atlantic Dr.

Katama (South) Beach

signs, *nobody* stops! With great caution, go straight ahead onto Lagoon Pond Road to Skiff Avenue, turn right, and ride to Edgartown Road. Cross over to the bike path on the right side for a 6-mile downhill ride to Main Street in Edgartown.

Landing at Oak Bluffs is simpler. As you leave the ferry, turn left onto Beach Road, which also has a fine paved bike path: 5 miles on the flat, along the shore of Nantucket Sound, to where it meets the 6-miler from Vineyard Haven at Edgartown's Main Street.

Exploring Edgartown will take a little ingenuity, because the town fathers and mothers have recently established definite routes for bikes, and with the use of signs such as ALL BIKES MUST TURN RIGHT (or LEFT) BIKES: DO NOT ENTER. But this is a very small town with only four principal streets—Water, Summer, School, and Pease Way—so try it this way: Ride into town on Main Street, following the directional signs reading BIKE ROUTE TO CHAPPY FERRY. They will take you to the slip for the On Time Ferry to Chappaquiddick. If you've never been there, the little 4-car-and-*beaucoup*-bicycles-capacity ferry runs continually, taking little more than a minute for the voyage. The fare is $3.00 round-trip for bike and rider.

The Public Wharf next to the ferry landing has an observation deck with a great view. When you are ready to leave this place, ride up Daggett Street to North Water Street. (If Daggett is one-way, you can walk your bike this short distance.) To your right is the Daggett House Inn, built in 1750 and open to the public. Turn right. From here to the end of the street are Martha's Vineyard's handsomest captains' houses. Several were built at an angle to afford views of homebound ships rounding Cape Poge. The chimneys, picket fences, door fans, and other well-crafted wood details contribute to the elegance of these houses, built in the early nineteenth century.

At the end of North Water Street, lock up your bike and walk to the lighthouse, and then turn left onto Starbuck Neck Road. Starbuck Neck Road comes to a T at Fuller Street. Turn left here and head back toward Main Street.

At Morse Street turn right and then immediately left on North Summer Street. On this street you'll pass the little red brick St. Andrew's Church, the Christine Pease House, and the Captain Henry

Holt House (1828), now a guest house. Take Summer past Main, Cook, and High streets to a T with Pease Point Way. Here you turn left and very soon are on Katama Road, with a bike path on its left.

Bear left at the fork with Edgartown Bay Road. At the fork with Town Lot Road, remain on Edgartown Bay Road. Circle around the point. The barrier beach can be seen from here. Proceed west to rejoin Katama Road. Turn left, heading toward Katama Beach. Your road forms a T with Atlantic Drive, which parallels Mattakesset Herring Creek. Katama Beach is a beautiful 3-mile-long white sand beach. There is surf on the ocean side of the barrier and there is saltwater pond swimming on the bay side.

When you're ready to leave the area, go west on Atlantic Drive. Turn right on Herring Creek Road, ride past the airfield and Crocker Road, and rejoin Katama Road. Ride up Katama Road until you come to South Water Street. There will be a sign here: ALL BIKES MUST TURN RIGHT. There's no use fighting City Hall, so turn right and then left at High Street, going up past South Summer Street to a right turn on School Street. Take School Street past Cook to Main Street, where you turn left. You are now bidding farewell to Edgartown, which has maintained the even tenor of its ways since the early nineteenth century.

Main Street will take you out to the crossroad where both bike paths meet. Take yours to wherever you came from. Godspeed and may the wind be at your back!

Vineyard Haven– Lambert's Cove (Martha's Vineyard)

Number of miles:	15.5
Approximate pedaling time:	2 hours
Terrain:	Hilly
Surface:	Good
Things to see:	Vineyard Haven, West Chop, Lambert's Cove Road, Seamen's Bethel, Williams Street houses, Cedar Tree Neck

With this ride you are going to see and get a feel for the agricultural heart of the island. But you'll first take a tour of West Chop and a residential section of Vineyard Haven and then head out to Lambert's Cove in what's called Up-Island. And why is it called Up-Island? Because the whaling ship captains called it that from their nautical way of describing the direction they were sailing in. When they were sailing west, the minutes of longitude went *up*; when sailing east, they went *down*. You are heading west—therefore Up-Island.

Start the ride at the ferry landing in Vineyard Haven. If you are on the island in the summer season, you will have company—lots of company—and since the number of visitors is large and the island is small, you would do better to leave your vehicle at Woods Hole and just bring yourself and your bike (or rent one across from the dock). But if you do bring your vehicle, hopefully you can park it in the town parking lot on Water Street, across from the Steamship Authority parking.

Facing away from the dock, turn left on Water Street and then right on Beach Street; then go uphill the short distance to Main, where you turn right. Main Street now goes uphill toward West Chop. As you climb, you can take in all of beautiful Vineyard Haven Harbor. The hill soon crests and you start a downhill run of nearly a

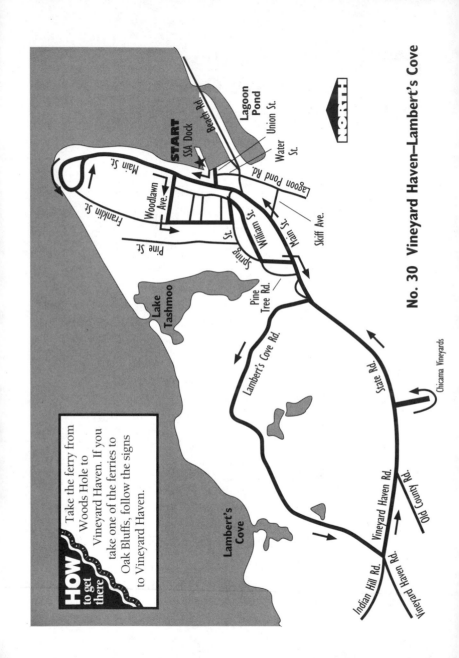

No. 30 Vineyard Haven–Lambert's Cove

NORTH

HOW to get there Take the ferry from Woods Hole to Vineyard Haven. If you take one of the ferries to Oak Bluffs, follow the signs to Vineyard Haven.

START

SSA Dock

Beach Rd.

Lagoon Pond

Union St.

Water St.

Lagoon Pond Rd.

Main St.

Woodlawn Ave.

Franklin St.

Pine St.

Spring St.

William St.

Main St.

Skiff Ave.

Pine Tree Rd.

Lake Tashmoo

Lambert's Cove Rd.

State Rd.

Chicama Vineyards

Lambert's Cove

Indian Hill Rd.

Vineyard Haven Rd.

Old County Rd.

Vineyard Haven Rd.

half-mile. At the bottom of the hill, Main Street changes its name to West Chop Avenue.

As you go out on the West Chop bluffs, the houses get larger. One mile farther on West Chop Avenue, which rolls up and down, you'll notice a BIKE ROUTE sign on the left side of the road. At the top of West Chop, there's an overlook of the ocean, complete with flagpole and bench. The bike route, which you follow, makes a loop to the left through West Chop woods. At the point where Franklin Street comes in from the right, you continue straight ahead, following the BIKE ROUTE sign. Within a short distance you will have completed the loop and will be back at West Chop Avenue, where you turn right.

Come back on West Chop Avenue to Woodlawn Avenue, the next street after the public library. You must turn right here because Main Street is one-way against you at this point. From Woodlawn turn left on Franklin Street. Ride to Spring Street and turn left. Go 1 block and turn right 135 degrees onto William. The WILLIAM street sign is on the corner to your left. Curve uphill to the right and stay on William until it tees with Pine Tree Road. Turn left. Pine Tree soon comes to a T at State Road at an angle, where you turn right, heading west, downhill on curving, rolling State Road.

In less than a half-mile, you should see a sign for LAMBERT'S COVE. Turn right at the sign, onto Lambert's Cove Road. If the sign is missing, there should at least be a sign on the left side reading GAY HEAD 17 VINEYARD HAVEN 2. You're now in horse country, with old farms and stone walls and a patch of forest now and again. One mile from the turn onto Lambert's Cove Road, start a nice downhill run. Just before this hill is the entrance to Cranberry Acres, one of three privately owned campgrounds open to the public.

In 0.5 mile you pass into West Tisbury and go abruptly uphill, then around a curve and down again. This is a hilly road but very scenic, with views of forests and open, flat areas on either side. Pass Duarte Pond on the left and then an old country cemetery on the right. In another 0.4 mile start a brief but steep uphill climb to beautiful little Lambert's Cove Methodist Church. Lambert's Cove Road curves around to the left, past Seth's Pond and up a 0.4-mile-long grade to the intersection with Vineyard Haven Road. Take a sharp left turn onto Vineyard Haven Road (State Road), heading back toward Vineyard Haven.

If you like to walk along nature trails, take a side trip here by turning right instead of left, going a short distance, and turning forty-five degrees right onto Indian Hill Road. Follow this road for 0.75 mile to the end. Just before the turnaround a sign on the right directs you to Vineyard Sound. Take this dirt road 1 mile to the Cedar Tree Neck Wildlife Sanctuary. No swimming or picnicking is permitted, but communing is encouraged.

Continue the ride on Vineyard Haven Road. Soon Old County Road comes in from the right and merges with Vineyard Haven Road. Bear left and continue on this well-paved road, which is now taking you through flat countryside. At this point start watching for a sign on your side of the road that will direct you to THE WINERY AT CHICAMA VINEYARDS. It may also say THIMBLE FARM. Turn off at the sign and ride down the lane to the place where in 1971 George Mathiesen and his family started with seventy-five vinifera vines and where today their winery produces 100,000 bottles a year. They have free tours and tastings daily from Memorial Day to Columbus Day and a shop selling their wines and herbed vinegars, jellies, and mustards prepared on the premises. Down the lane a piece is Thimble Farm, with pick-your-own or boxed strawberries and raspberries in season.

Back on State Road, in about a mile you'll pass Lambert's Cove Road on the left and continue on into Vineyard Haven as Old County Road changes to State Road and then to South Main Street as it curves downward into town. When you get to the fork with Main Street, bear left on Main. If you want to get back to the ferry dock, ride past Spring and Center streets on the left and turn right on Union Street.

Vineyard Haven–Martha's Vineyard State Forest

Number of miles:	18
Approximate pedaling time:	2½ hours
Terrain:	Flat
Surface:	Good
Things to see:	Martha's Vineyard State Forest, American Youth Hostel, The Winery at Chicama Vineyards, Thimble Farm, Vineyard Haven

Martha's Vineyard is almost triangular in shape, about 20 miles wide, east to west, and 10 miles long, north to south—not a very large piece of land. Its international reputation as an ideal place to spend one's precious vacation time poses a real question as to whether the island will be able to keep its superb natural beauty and still entertain hordes of visitors, many of whom fall in love with it and want to become full-time or summer residents. Fortunately, there have been farsighted people in the past and still today who have founded organizations to preserve as much of the island in its natural state as possible, such as the Land Bank, which is funded by a 2 percent tax on real estate transactions. More than 11,000 acres, almost one-fifth of the island, are now conservation land, and more is being acquired every year.

This ride will take you to Martha's Vineyard State Forest, which has 4,000 of those conservation acres within its boundaries. It starts from Vineyard Haven, from the Steamship Authority dock. Once you have gotten off the boat with your bike, or have taken it off your vehicle, or have rented one a hop, skip, and jump away on the corner of Union and Water streets, and you are all set to ride, turn left on Water Street and go the short distance to the intersection called Five Corners. Here you will go straight across onto Lagoon Pond Road,

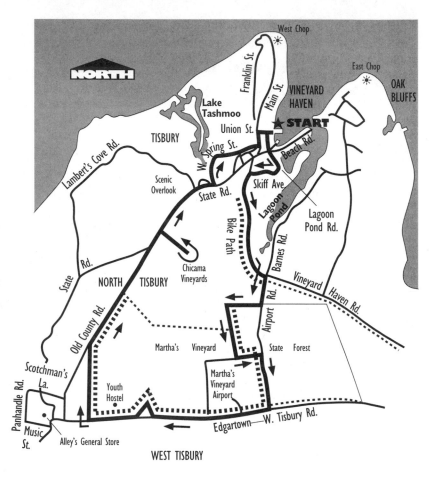

No. 31 Vineyard Haven

which turns right at the edge of Lagoon Pond and then left onto Skiff Avenue, which soon comes to a T with Edgartown– Vineyard Haven Road, where you turn left. Ride across the road to the bike path, a two-way path for bicycles and pedestrians. In approximately 2 miles you'll come to the intersection of Edgartown–Vineyard Haven Road and Airport Road/Barnes Road, Airport to the right and Barnes to the left. Turn right and go down Airport Road about 0.5 mile to an entrance to the state forest bike trail on your right. Turn onto the bike trail, which will take you on a 5-mile circuit of the forest. It turns ninety degrees left in approximately 0.75 mile, then continues straight ahead, where a branch of it comes in from the right, to the boundary of the Martha's Vineyard Airport. Here you turn left and go about 0.5 mile to another ninety-degree turn, this time to the right. From this point you have a straight path for about 1 mile. The path parallels Airport Road, which you can catch a glimpse of through the trees now and then, off to your left. At the end of the mile, you will come to a T, where you turn right. You are now heading west, parallel to Edgartown–West Tisbury Road.

In about 1 mile the path makes a short triangular jog to the right just before you come to the American Youth Hostel off to your left. If the hostel is not open when you arrive, you can still rest and have lunch at a picnic table under a shady tree, as I did one fine day in June. A half-mile down the path from the hostel, you can ride the short distance to the Edgartown–West Tisbury Road, go right, and take a 0.5-mile detour to the center of West Tisbury, with its white, steepled church and Alley's General Store—as described in Ride 32. The bike path now turns north and goes up to and then parallels Old County Road for close to 3 miles, to the point where the ride and the bike path part company and you continue north on Old County Road. As soon as State Road comes in from the left, start watching for the sign for The Winery at Chicama Vineyards; from the sign the winery is down a short winding lane to your right. If you didn't check it out on Ride 30, take a look now if you have the time. Once back on State Road, you'll be turning off on West Spring Street after the Lake Tashmoo scenic overlook for the run back to Main Street in Vineyard Haven.

West Tisbury–Menemsha
(Martha's Vineyard)

Number of miles: 16
Approximate pedaling time: 2 hours
Terrain: Definitely hilly and curving
Surface: Fair
Things to see: Menemsha Harbor, village of West
Tisbury, Chilmark Center, seascapes

With this ride we're going to point our bicycles southwest and go Up-Island, farther out, along country roads that meander through woods and quiet farmland and then down into another world, the tiny but very busy fishing village of Menemsha. West Tisbury has been a sheep farming region for 200 years, and it remains one. It has horse farms and produce farms, too, and its center is very much the archetypical New England country village, complete with handsome white church and large country store.

If you have come to the Vineyard without a vehicle, you can get to the starting place at the Y intersection of State (or Vineyard Haven) Road, North Road, and South Road by taking State Street out of Vineyard Haven. You go down North Road, following the arrow to Menemsha. If you are carrying bikes on a car, you can go down the left fork, South Road, about 1.5 miles to West Tisbury and park near the General Store and Post Office. Once on your bike, ride back up to the Y and turn left onto North Road, following the arrow that points the way to Menemsha. You're on a lovely curving road that goes through wooded areas of trees and thickets but also provides some views of walled pastureland and of Vineyard Sound. About 3 miles from the fork, you will pass Tea Lane, a tree-lined, narrow dirt road, to your left. This section of road continues to be quite hilly. About 2 miles

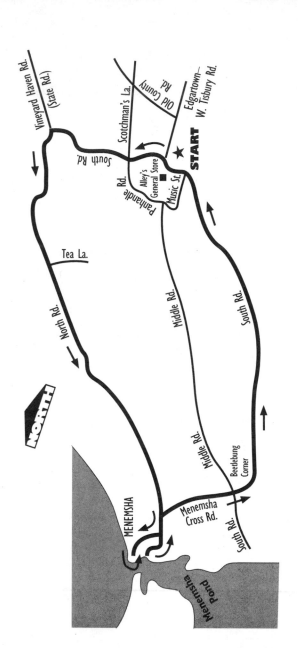

Refer to the first section of the ride itself.

No. 32 West Tisbury–Menemsha

from Tea Lane, the road crests, providing a vista of Menemsha Pond. Soon you will go sharply downhill, past the sign to Gay Head and Chilmark, into the tiny fishing hamlet of Menemsha; there are several docks, fishing shacks clinging to the littoral, small boats, and large fishing vessels. You'll also spot boats for charter and a fine anchorage for visiting pleasure craft. (If all of this seems strangely familiar to you, not to worry; you probably saw the movie *Jaws,* which used Menemsha for location shots.) After you go out on the dirt road alongside the inlet to Menemsha Pond, come back and turn left at the first paved road and go out to Dutcher's Dock, passing a couple of art galleries; stopping for a snack and a look at the village fish markets, where everything from lobster to eels can be purchased fresh daily; and proceeding on to the little public beach.

When you're ready, return to North Road and go up the steep hill to the intersection with Menemsha Cross Road, which may not be so marked but should have a sign GAYHEAD–CHILMARK. Turn right and proceed about 1 mile to Beetlebung Corner with its handsome Methodist church and fire and police stations.

Beetlebung is the old Islander name for the tupelo trees you'll see here, and the "Corner" is the intersection of Menemsha Cross Road, Middle Road to your left, and South Road, which is both to your right and straight ahead.

You go straight ahead on South Road, which turns sharply left in a few hundred yards to begin the eastward leg toward West Tisbury. All along this portion of the ride are views of ponds, hills, the ocean, and the stone walls of old sheep farms; it is also hilly, and, combined with the Up-Island's typical narrow, curvy roads, it spells caution.

In about 3 miles a long downhill run offers an expansive view of moors, dunes, and ocean. This will be followed by a gradual uphill grade before you arrive in the village of West Tisbury in about 2 miles. Here you'll find a grange and a Congregational church on the left, an art gallery (with Picassoesque sculptures in the garden) on the right, and fine old white frame houses.

Sir Joshua Slocum, who was the first to circumnavigate the globe alone in his motorless sloop *Spray,* made his home here for many years before being lost at sea in 1907. His house can be reached by taking a short detour up South Road and then right onto Edgartown–West Tisbury Road. The house is on the right.

Alley's General Store in West Tisbury is well worth your time. You can get an apple or a candy bar before loading your bike on the car—if that's the way you came—or you can continue up South Road, past the intersection with Edgartown–West Tisbury Road. Soon there'll be a sharp left—with a cemetery straight ahead for those who came to Martha's Vineyard and never left. You will cross Mill Brook and soon be back at the Y with North Road and State Road, which will take you back to Vineyard Haven.

Gay Head
(Martha's Vineyard)

Number of miles:	11.2
Approximate pedaling time:	1½ hours
Terrain:	Definitely hilly and curving
Surface:	Fair
Things to see:	Gay Head Cliffs and Lighthouse, Menemsha Pond, Elizabeth Islands

Gay Head is not a village or a town. It has been an Indian reservation since 1987, when the Wampanoag tribe won the right to be the guardians of 420 acres that include the Gay Head Cliffs—a National Historic Landmark and part of the Gay Head Indian Reservation.

Start your ride at the mile-long Gay Head Cliffs at Martha's Vineyard's westernmost tip, about 19 miles from Vineyard Haven. There are public facilities located at this National Historic Landmark, as well as snack bars and souvenir shops. These glacial cliffs, millions of years old, are made of multilayered clays of different colors. Paleontologists have uncovered bones of ancient whales, horses, and camels in the area. One couldn't tire of the views afforded from this site: the cliffs themselves, whose clays color the water crashing into them; the western seascape of the lighthouse; the Chilmark hills; and the ponds, dunes, and beaches of Martha's Vineyard.

When you leave the cliffs, bear left on the one-way loop and then turn right on Moshup Trail. Head downhill toward the water. The Gay Head town beach is on the right. Summer houses are perched randomly among the hills and dunes, and the dunes are covered with grasses like bear's fur. Low shrubs, bushes, and stunted trees provide the vegetation at Gay Head. The effect is rather desolate but also unique. Moshup Trail parallels the coast. About a mile from the cliffs,

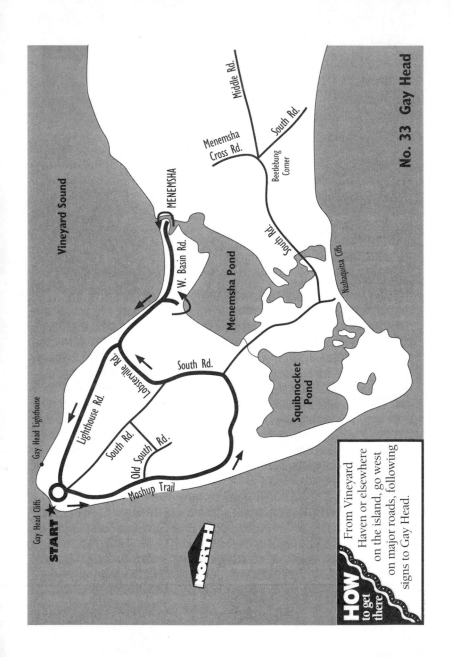

Vineyard Sound

Gay Head Cliffs
Gay Head Lighthouse
START ★

MENEMSHA

W. Basin Rd.

Menemsha Pond

Lighthouse Rd.

Lobsterville Rd.

South Rd.

South Rd.

Old South Rd.

Moshup Trail

Squibnocket Pond

South Rd.

Nashaquitsa Cliffs

Menemsha Cross Rd.

Beetlebung Corner

South Rd.

Middle Rd.

NORTH

HOW to get there

From Vineyard Haven or elsewhere on the island, go west on major roads, following signs to Gay Head.

No. 33 Gay Head

Old South Road enters from the left. About 2 miles after this junction, a long grade of about 0.7 mile begins. Stop occasionally for resting and viewing Zachs Cliffs, Long Beach, Squibnocket Pond, and other sights.

At South Road, where there's a stop sign but maybe not a street sign, turn left. The road soon crests and then continues its up-and-down formations, continuing to snake around as well. At the sign LOBSTERVILLE TOWN BEACH, turn right onto Lobsterville Road (there once was a fishing community here by this name). Enjoy a great downhill ride here as you head toward Vineyard Sound. In a little over a mile, Lighthouse Road joins you from the left, but you continue straight ahead and then bear left on West Basin Road. Follow this road to its end, with Vineyard Sound on your left and Menemsha Pond on your right. An Adriatic-like pebbly beach is all along this road amid sand dunes. Directly ahead at the end of the road is Menemsha Bight, an inlet of the sound.

You face the village of Menemsha across the bight, but you can't get there from here. (Visit the hamlet on the West Tisbury–Menemsha ride, page 119.) Menemsha's harbor is beautifully protected and so is full of fishing and pleasure craft year-round.

Turn around and head back up West Basin Road. Take a brief detour down to the pond's edge and the public landing when you come upon a road going off to the left. Return to West Basin Road and proceed straight ahead to its intersection with Lobsterville and Lighthouse Road. Turn right and head west on Lighthouse Road. Summer houses also dot the terrain on this side of Gay Head. After about 2 miles on Lighthouse Road, you'll arrive at the Gay Head Lighthouse, built in 1952. The first lighthouse on this site was built in 1799. Continue to the Gay Head Cliffs and the end of the ride.

34 Combination:
Vineyard Haven–Lambert's Cove & West Tisbury–Menemsha (Martha's Vineyard)

Number of miles:	35
Approximate pedaling time:	4½ hours
Terrain:	Hilly
Surface:	Good
Things to see:	Vineyard Haven, West Chop, Lambert's Cove Road, Seamen's Bethel, Williams Street houses, Cedar Tree Neck, Menemsha Harbor, village of West Tisbury, Chilmark Center, seascapes

The nine rides on Martha's Vineyard cover most of the island and can be ridden one at a time or in combinations, depending on such things as the time of year (days are longer in summer), whether you came by car or bike alone, whether you've come for the day or a longer stay, where you are staying, and, when all's said and done, how well you feel.

If you're game, try putting two rides together by starting out from Vineyard Haven on the Vineyard Haven–Lambert's Cove ride (Ride 30); when you get to the point where Lambert's Cove Road meets Vineyard Haven Road, go right instead of left onto the latter and ride about 1.5 miles to the Y with South and North roads. Turn right onto North Road and make the complete 16-mile circuit of the West Tisbury–Menemsha ride (Ride 32).

When you arrive back at the Y with South and North roads, bear right and go back the 1.5 miles to the junction of Vineyard Haven and Lambert's Cove roads, bear to the right, and do the last half of the Vineyard Haven–Lambert's Cove ride, back into Vineyard Haven.

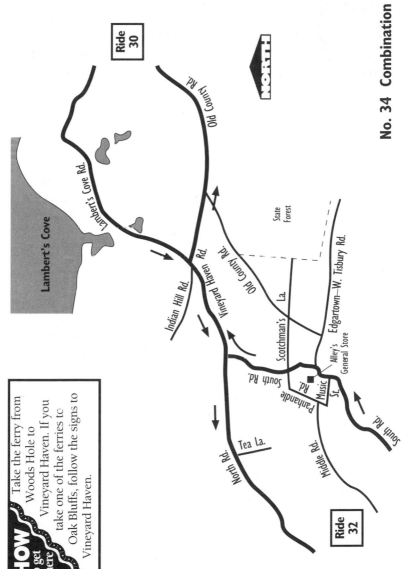

HOW to get there Take the ferry from Woods Hole to Vineyard Haven. If you take one of the ferries to Oak Bluffs, follow the signs to Vineyard Haven.

Lambert's Cove

Ride 30

Ride 32

NORTH

No. 34 Combination

Lambert's Cove Rd.

Old County Rd.

Indian Hill Rd.

Vineyard Haven Rd.

Old County Rd.

State Forest

Scotchman's La.

Edgartown—W. Tisbury Rd.

Alley's General Store

South Rd.

Panhandle Rd.

Music St.

Middle Rd.

South Rd.

North Rd.

Tea La.

35 Combination:
Oak Bluffs/Vineyard Haven–Edgartown & Chappaquiddick (Martha's Vineyard)

Number of miles:	28
Approximate pedaling time:	4 hours
Terrain:	Flat to moderately hilly
Surface:	Fair
Things to see:	Joseph Sylvia State Beach, Wesleyan Grove Campground, East Chop, the Flying Horses Carousel, Felix Neck Wildlife Sanctuary, Ocean Park, East Beach, Cape Poge Light, Mytoi, Wasque Wildlife Preservation Area, Dyke Bridge, On Time Ferry

This combination ride will start out in either Oak Bluffs or Vineyard Haven and follow the route of the Oak Bluffs/Vineyard Haven–Edgartown ride (Ride 27) to the point where Beach Road joins Edgartown Road, a short distance from the center of Edgartown. Instead of turning sharply left, continue straight into Edgartown. You'll be on Main Street. Follow it and the signs to the CHAPPY FERRY down to North Water Street; turn left to Daggett, turn right, and you will see the little three-car ferry. It's called the On Time Ferry because, not having a schedule, it's always on time.

Now you are at the beginning of the Chappaquiddick ride (Ride 28). When you return on the ferry, make your way back to the junction of Edgartown–Vineyard Haven Road and Beach Road, which is also called the Edgartown–Oak Bluffs Road; bear right and continue the Oak Bluffs/Vineyard Haven–Edgartown ride on the bike path along the ocean to Oak Bluffs.

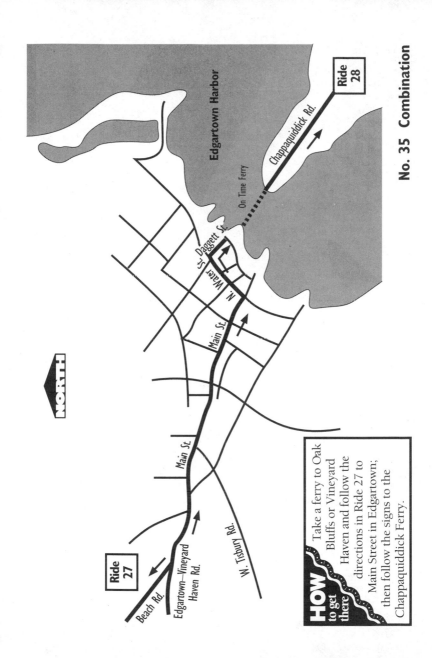

North

Ride 27

Beach Rd.
Edgartown–Vineyard Haven Rd.
Main St.
W. Tisbury Rd.
Main St.
N. Water St.
Daggett St.

On Time Ferry

Edgartown Harbor

Chappaquiddick Rd.

Ride 28

HOW to get there Take a ferry to Oak Bluffs or Vineyard Haven and follow the directions in Ride 27 to Main Street in Edgartown; then follow the signs to the Chappaquiddick Ferry.

No. 35 Combination

36 Nantucket Town–Surfside (Nantucket)

Number of miles:	10.2
Approximate pedaling time:	2 hours
Terrain:	Flat to moderately hilly
Surface:	Good to excellent
Things to see:	The marvelous town of Nantucket itself, the Peter Foulger Museum, the Whaling Museum, Surfside Beach

From the middle of the eighteenth century to the middle of the nineteenth, Nantucket was the leading whaling port in the world. From the busy harbor, ships set off for the whaling grounds of first the Atlantic and then the Pacific and returned loaded to the gunwales with barrels of whale oil, which were off-loaded and trundled to refineries and candle factories. It was boom time, and while it lasted, large fortunes were made and magnificent houses built by the whaling merchants and the whaling ships' captains, who, with their seamen, endured the hard and dangerous voyages that kept them from home and hearth for as long as five years. The whaling merchant Joseph Starbuck (now there's a name to conjure by!) built three identical red brick mansions side by side on Upper Main Street for his three sons.

Today Nantucket has managed to retain a great deal of its character, partly because of its distance from the mainland—30 miles out in the open ocean—but mostly because of the foresight and persistence of people who worked hard to ensure that Nantucket would keep all that makes it special. The designation of the entire island as a National Historical District was obtained through legislation in the 1950s. Now any change in the outward appearance of a structure must adhere to a strict code. Nantucket today looks much the way it did 150 years ago.

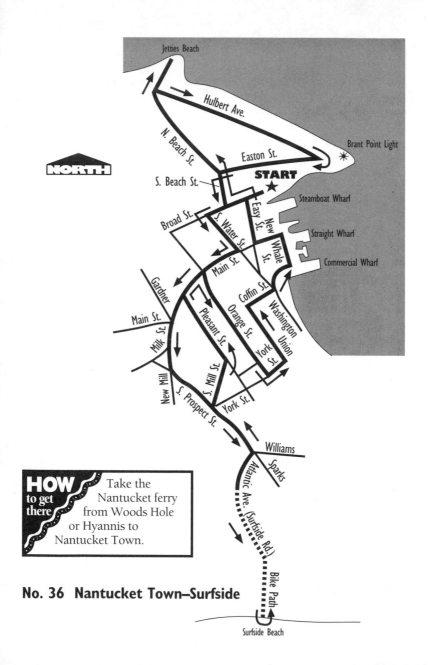

Jetties Beach

Hulbert Ave.

Brant Point Light

N. Beach St.

Easton St.

NORTH

S. Beach St.

START

Steamboat Wharf

Broad St.

S. Water St.

Easy St.

New Whale St.

Straight Wharf

Commercial Wharf

Main St.

Gardner

Coffin St.

Main St.

Pleasant St.

Orange St.

Washington

Milk St.

Union

New Mill

S. Mill St.

York St.

York St.

S. Prospect St.

Williams

HOW to get there Take the Nantucket ferry from Woods Hole or Hyannis to Nantucket Town.

Atlantic Ave. (Surfside Rd.)

Sparks

Bike Path

No. 36 Nantucket Town–Surfside

Surfside Beach

So, let's go exploring. Start the ride at Steamboat Wharf, where the ferry comes in. There are two bike shops here in case you need supplies or repairs or want to rent a bike. Go up Broad Street past Easy Street (which is one-way coming from your left). Ride past Beach Street, the Peter Foulger Museum, and the Whaling Museum.

Turn left on South Water Street and then right on Main Street. Main is paved with small, irregular cobblestones dating from the 1830s. These stones had served as ballast; they were laid to prevent wagons laden with oil casks from sinking into the sand. They were a boon in the 1800s, but they are a bane to cyclists today.

Go up Main Street to the bank and bear left. Where Gardner comes in from the right, Main Street goes right forty-five degrees, but you bear left on Milk Street, passing Vestal on the right. At the fork bear left on New Mill, which is one-way against you, so walk your bike. The next street is Prospect; turn left. Watch for street signs. (Since the houses are built close together, down to the edge of the narrow sidewalks, the street signs are often hung on the sides of the houses.)

At the fork bear right onto South Prospect Street and go about 0.25 mile to the intersection of Prospect, Williams, Sparks, and Atlantic Avenue (also called Surfside Road). The sign says HOSPITAL and SURFSIDE. Turn almost ninety degrees right onto Atlantic. Within a short distance, across from the Nantucket High School, you will find a bike path on the right side of Atlantic Avenue. Cross over it and enjoy a 2.5-mile ride to the beach, one of the island's most popular, with lifeguard, snack bar, and bathhouse.

After a surfeit of sun and surf, return along the same route to the Old Mill, on the corner of South Prospect, York, and South Mill streets.

Turn right around the site of the Old Mill onto South Mill Street with the mill on your left. This is the one survivor of the four that originally stood on the hill, grinding corn. Go downhill on South Mill Street. Turn left at the bottom of the hill at the T intersection with Pleasant Street. Proceed along Pleasant Street to Main, where you turn right. On the corner, at 96 Main Street, is the Hawden-Satler House. The three Georgian brick mansions across the street are identical. They were built between 1836 and 1838 by Joseph Starbuck, a whaler, for his three sons. The middle house is still inhabited by descendants of the original owner. A Starbuck whaling ship set two records in 1859: It returned with 6,000 barrels of oil after a five-year voyage!

At Orange Street turn right. There may not be a sign for Orange Street, but there will be a series of signposts, reading SURFSIDE—BIKE PATH, POLPIS—WAUWINET, HOSPITAL—AIRPORT, and SIASCONSET BIKE PATH. More houses of whaling ship captains line Orange Street than any other street in the world. Go to York Street, turn left and left again onto Union Street, and head back toward the center of town. At Coffin Street turn right and go to Washington. Turn left and then immediately right and head toward Commercial (Swain's) Wharf.

Lock your bike to any handy post here and walk around the three public wharves, Commercial, Straight, and Old South. Commercial fishing and scalloping boats still come and go.

From here proceed around the parking area on New Whale Street, turn up Main, and then go along Easy Street 4 short blocks to Broad. If you have time for a swim, turn left on Broad and then right onto South Beach Street. Go 3 blocks to the stop sign at Easton Street. Jog across to North Beach Street. Head up a slight hill. Beyond the Bird Sanctuary on the left, bear right where the sign says JETTIES BEACH, the main public beach on the island. There is a gently sloping beach on one side and a shallow beach for children on the other. There is a lifeguard, a bathhouse, and a restaurant.

Leaving Jetties Beach, take the first left, Hulbert Avenue. Follow it to Brant Point Light. Go right, out to the point. Come back and continue straight ahead on Easton to the intersection with North and South Beach streets. Turn left onto South Beach and proceed back to Steamboat Wharf.

Madaket (Nantucket)

Number of miles:	15.7
Approximate pedaling time:	2 hours
Terrain:	Flat to gently rolling
Surface:	Very good; bike path for most of the route
Things to see:	The western half of Nantucket with its moors, Dionis Beach, Madaket Harbor and Beach, Hither Creek, Eel Point

If you are akin to most of those who come to Nantucket, you've come to find a place that looks and feels different: quieter, with a slower pace and rhythm than the city and the century you have just stepped out of. Nantucket is such a place. This ride will take you through Nantucket Town and out to the moors, where, if the breeze is right, you can catch the scents of heather, bayberry, and wild roses as they waft across the moors.

Start in front of the Peter Foulger Museum on Broad Street. Turn left on South Water Street to Main Street. Turn right and continue up cobbled Main, which becomes Madaket Road. In short order you will come to Canton Circle with a flagpole in the center where Main Street, Lowell Place, Quaker, and Madaket roads meet. On the left side there is a great bike path that runs all the way to Madaket, a distance of approximately 5 miles.

About 1.5 miles from Canton Circle, you'll reach Eel Point Road and a sign saying DIONIS BEACH. If you are in the mood for beautiful sand dunes, a lifeguard, rest rooms, and gentle surf, turn right. The beach is down the road about 0.75 mile. When you are ready, come

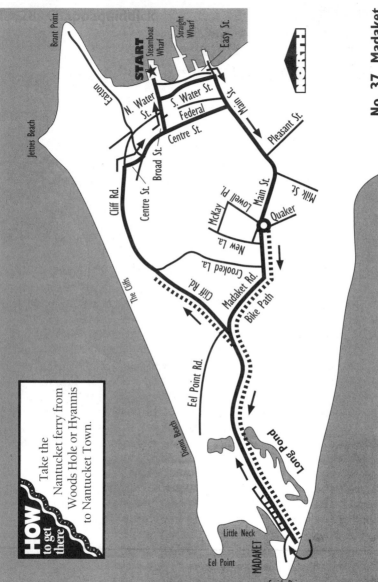

No. 37 Madaket

back to the Madaket Road bike path and continue across the heath—or moor, as the islanders call it—toward the western end of the island.

In about 2 miles you'll cross over an inlet between the two halves of Long Pond, and then the road and path turn left and go straight to Madaket Beach, which is on the Atlantic side and is another splendid beach.

When you come back from the beach, turn left and go across the little bridge over the westernmost end of Hither Creek to Smith Point on the left or Jackson Point on the right; then come back to Madaket Road and turn back to the left. When you come to a sign that reads HITHER CREEK BOATYARD or CAMBRIDGE STREET, turn left. This will take you to Little Neck, a Nantucket Conservation Foundation property open to the public.

If you have time, you can also turn left when you reach Warren's Landing Road and take this dirt road out 1.5 miles to Eel Point, a 128-acre wildlife reservation. Coming back to Madaket Road and the bike path, turn left once more and ride back toward Nantucket Town on the bike path, taking in the sights and scents of the moor from the opposite direction. When you arrive at the intersection of Madaket, Eel Point, and Cliff roads, cross over to the bike path alongside Cliff Road. This new bike path ends in about a mile; you continue on Cliff Road, which takes you fairly close to the cliffs along the north shore of the island. It's a hilly road but in this direction more downhill than up. About a mile from the end of the bike path, Cliff Road curves right to a Y, with Centre Street to the right and North Water Street to the left. You go right onto Centre Street and ride down to Broad Street.

Siasconset (Nantucket)

Number of miles:	26 or 22.5
Approximate pedaling time:	2¾ hours
Terrain:	Flat to moderately hilly
Surface:	Good to poor
Things to see:	Nantucket Harbor, Wauwinet, Sankaty Head Light, Siasconset, Siasconset Beach

Before you begin this ride, a wise decision would be to visit the Museum of Nantucket History in Nantucket Town on Straight Wharf, housed in a restored warehouse that once stored whaling ship supplies. Its visual and audio displays and dioramas and its live demonstrations of early island crafts will give you a good perspective for the sights you will see as you ride around the island.

The ride starts at the foot of Main Street in front of the Pacific Club, which was formed in 1859 by a group of former Pacific whaling ship masters for "yarning" together. The building is now home of the Nantucket Chamber of Commerce.

Unless you have a hybrid or mountain bike, walk up the square (because of the cobblestones); just before reaching the Pacific National Bank, turn left onto Orange Street. There may not be an OR-ANGE STREET sign, but there will be a series of signposts, reading SURFSIDE–BIKE PATH, POLPIS–WAUWINET, HOSPITAL–AIRPORT, and SIASCON-SET BIKE PATH. The latter is the destination for which you are heading. About 1 mile from the start, you will come to the Milestone Rotary, identified by a sign: POLPIS SIASCONSET. Go around to the left and onto the Milestone Bike Path, which starts here. This path will take you straight down to the only other town on Nantucket, Siasconset,

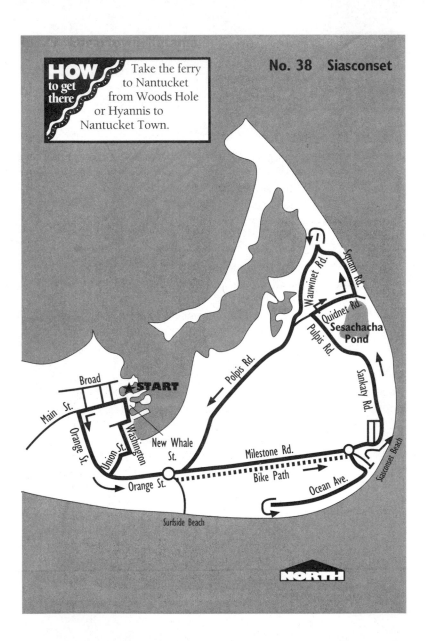

HOW to get there — Take the ferry to Nantucket from Woods Hole or Hyannis to Nantucket Town.

Broad
Main St.
★START
Orange St.
Union St.
Washington
New Whale St.
Orange St.
Surfside Beach
Milestone Rd.
Bike Path
Ocean Ave.
Polpis Rd.
Wauwinet Rd.
Squam Rd.
Quidnet Rd.
Sesachacha Pond
Pulpis Rd.
Sankaty Rd.
Siasconset Beach

NORTH

called Sconset for short. The bike path is 6 miles long, most of it gently downhill. Just before you reach Sconset, about 5.5 miles from the Milestone Rotary, look for a sign on the left pointing to the Milestone Bog, more than 200 acres of a working cranberry bog that has been in cultivation since 1857. If you come in late September, the harvest will have begun and continues for six weeks, seven days a week, from sunrise to sunset. The bog is flooded and fills with the floating red cranberries. It's a sight not to be missed!

You are now getting your first look at Nantucket's open heath or moor with its great variety of wildflowers, bayberry, scrub oaks, pine groves, and purple scotch heather. The first settlers found a treeless island. The Coffin brothers imported 30,000 pine trees in 1851 and planted them in these outlying areas. About 0.5 mile after the bike path ends, you will come to a rotary that is distinguished by a flagpole made from a ship's spar. Here you go around to the right, uphill on Ocean Avenue, also called Beach Road, which goes along a bluff overlooking the Atlantic Ocean. On the right side are Nantucket's larger summer homes. The view to the left is spectacular! You can ride out as far as the Coast Guard Loran Station before turning around, or you can turn around whenever you like and come back. Just before the rotary take a hairpin turn downhill and around to the right under the footbridge to Sconset Beach. There are bike racks and miles of beach stretching in either direction.

When you have picnicked or just rested, come back under the footbridge to the rotary, where you turn right and go into the town of Sconset with its doll-size cottages. Originally fishing shacks, they were enlarged to their present size in the eighteenth century when the wives of the fishermen decided to join them. Turn left on Broadway to the Y with Sankaty Road; turn right, heading north. Continue on Sankaty for about 2.5 miles, past Sesachacha Pond on the right, until it makes a T with Quidnet Road. Turn right onto Quidnet. (If you're getting tired or hungry—or both—you can cut 3.5 miles off the ride by continuing left on Sankaty Road.) In just about a mile, you will come to a stop sign and a sandy unpaved road coming in from the left. There is a sign on the left that reads THIS IS AN ABUTTER'S ROAD. PROCEED AT YOUR OWN RISK. This is Squam Road. Turn left; ride 2 miles on this narrow dirt/sand road, with the ocean on your right and Squam swamp on your left. It's a bit tricky on high-pressure, narrow-width tires, but it is navigable. A twenty-one-speed hybrid mountain/road bike would take it in stride.

Squam Road ends at Wauwinet Road, where you turn left and roll up and down it until it joins Polpis Road at a Y intersection. Bear right onto Polpis and ride through the moors for 4.5 miles until you come to Milestone Road. Cross over to the other side of Milestone to ride up to the rotary on the bike path. At the rotary turn right onto Orange Street. When you get to Union Street, turn right and follow it around to Francis Street. Turn right and then left onto Washington, which skirts South Beach.

At the point where Washington bears left at the fork with Candle Street, Washington becomes one-way against you. Turn right ninety degrees onto Commercial (or Swain's) Wharf just before the fork and then left on New Whale to tour the wharf area before ending your ride.

Bike Rental Centers

Cape Cod

Brewster
Brewster Bicycle Rental, 414 Underpass Road, Brewster, MA (508) 896–8149

Rail Trail Bike Shop, 302 Underpass Road, Brewster, MA (508) 896–8200

Idle Times Bike Shop, Nickerson State Park, Route 6A, Brewster, MA (508) 896–9242

Eastham
Little Capistrano Bike Shop, Salt Pond Road, Eastham, MA (508) 255–6515

Falmouth
Corner Cycle, 39 North Main Street, Falmouth, MA (508) 540–4195

Bill's Bike Shop, 847 E. Main Street, Falmouth, MA (508) 548–7979

Falmouth Heights
Holiday Cycles, 465 Grand Avenue, Falmouth Heights, MA (508) 540–3549

Harwich Port
Doctor Gravity's Kite Shop, 564 Route 28, Harwich Port, MA (508) 430–0437

Hyannis
Cove Cycles, 223 Barnstable Road, Hyannis, MA (508) 771–6155

North Eastham
Idle Times Bike Shop, Route 6, North Eastham, MA (508) 255–8281

North Falmouth
Art's Bike Shop, 75 Country Road, North Falmouth, MA (508)
563–7379

Orleans
Cape Cod Ski, Bike & Scuba, Route 6A, Orleans, MA (508) 255–7547

Provincetown
Arnold's, 329 Commercial Street, Provincetown, MA (508) 487–0844

Sandwich
Full Cycle, 7 Merchant Square, Sandwich, MA (508) 888–8445

South Wellfleet
Black Duck Sports Shop, Main Street, South Wellfleet, MA (508)
349–9801

South Yarmouth
The Outdoor Shop, 50 Long Pond Drive, South Yarmouth, MA (508)
394–3819

West Yarmouth
All Right Bike & Mower Shop, 627 Main Street, West Yarmouth, MA
(508) 771–8100

Martha's Vineyard

Edgartown
R. W. Cutler, Main Street, Edgartown, MA (508) 627–4052

Oak Bluffs
Anderson's, Grant Avenue Extension, Oak Bluffs, MA (508) 693–9346

Vineyard Haven

Cycle Works, State Road, Vineyard Haven, MA (508) 693–6966

Martha's Vineyard Scooter & Bike, Union Street, Vineyard Haven, MA
 (508) 693–0782

Nantucket

Cook's Cycle Shop, 6 South Beach Street, Nantucket, MA (508)
 228–0800

Fun Rentals, South Beach Street, Nantucket, MA (508) 228–4049

Holiday Cycle, 4 Chester, Nantucket, MA (508) 228–3644

Holiday Cycle, 135 Old South Road, Nantucket, MA (508) 228–1525

Nantucket Bike Shop, Steamboat Wharf, Nantucket, MA (508)
 228–1999

Young's Bicycle Shop, Steamboat Wharf, Nantucket, MA (508)
 228–1151 (year-round)

About the Author

Edwin Mullen is a "Clamdigger." He qualified for that title by being born on City Island, a tiny island that sits just off the coast of the Bronx borough of New York City. Drafted into the army at age eighteen, he survived a brief stint as a twin-engine bomber pilot in Italy.

He has been an actor, a producer, a purchasing agent for Yale University, and now, contentedly retired from the latter, a freelance writer and actor.